GENOCIDE IN
RWANDA

A COLLECTIVE
MEMORY

Edited by
John A. Berry and Carol Pott Berry

HOWARD UNIVERSITY PRESS
WASHINGTON, DC
1999

Howard University Press, Washington, DC 20001

Manufactured in the United States of America

This book is printed on acid-free paper.

10 9 8 7 6 5 4 3 2 1

Library of Congress Cataloging-in-Publication Data

Genocide in Rwanda : a collective memory / edited by
    John A. Berry and Carol Pott Berry.
        p.   cm.
    Based on material presented at a conference held
Jan. 19–20, 1995, Kigali, Rwanda.
    Includes bibliographical references (p.   ) and index.
    ISBN 0-88258-202-X
    1. Genocide—Rwanda—History—20th century.
2. Rwanda—Politics and government. 3. Rwanda—Ethnic
relations—History—20th century. 4. Tutsi (African people)—
Crimes against—Rwanda—History—20th century. 5. Hutu
(African people)—Rwanda—Politics and government.
I. Berry, John A., 1963-   . II. Berry, Carol Pott, 1964–   .
DT450.435.G47   1999
967.57104—dc21   99-10995
                                                          CIP

*This book is dedicated to
the memory of our friends and colleagues
and to the hundreds of thousands of Rwandans
who were killed in the genocide simply for being born a Tutsi
or for opposing a dictatorial regime.*

CONTENTS

PREFACE

Genocide in Rwanda attempts to record the words and opinions of individuals who experienced the genocide. The editors and funder of this book neither adopt as true, nor endorse, the words recorded herein.

This book is based upon material presented at the "Genocide: A Collective Memory" conference in Kigali, Rwanda, 19 and 20 January 1995.

Contributors (*in alphabetical order*)

Lise Boudreaux, Protection Officer, International Committee of the Red Cross
Dr. Maurice Bucagu, Director, Rwandan National Office for Population
François Byarhumwanzi, Director, Human Rights League of the Great Lakes
    Region, Rwandan Association for the Defense of Human Rights
Lieutenant Jean Marie Cameron, Liaison Officer, Rwandan Patriotic Army
Frederick Gatera, Program Officer, Austrian Relief Program
Faustin Kagame, Journalist

Thomas Kamilindi, Journalist, Radio Agatasha
Major Don MacNeil, Liaison Officer, United Nations Assistance Mission for
     Rwanda
Dr. Paulan Muswahili, Professor, National University of Rwanda
Jean Mutabaruka, Professor, National University of Rwanda
Lazare Nazaro, Civil Servant, Ministry of Rehabilitation and Social Integration
Dr. Jean Damescene Ndayambaje, Professor, National University of Rwanda
Emmanuel Ngomiraronka, Director, Hope Unlimited
Alphonse Marie Nkubito, former Minister of Justice, Government of Rwanda
Agnès Ntamabyaliro, Minister of Justice, Government of Rwanda in exile
Maurice Nyberg, Investigations Officer, Special Investigations Unit, United
     Nations Human Rights Field Operation
Charles Petrie, Deputy Director, United Nations Rwanda Emergency
     Operation
Major Frank Rusagara, Public Affairs Officer, Rwandan Patriotic Army
Andreas Schiess, Chief, Special Investigations Unit, United Nations Human
     Rights Field Operation
Alain Sigg, Public Affairs Officer, United Nations International Criminal
     Tribunal for Rwanda
Jeanne Kadalika Uwonkunda, Director, PROFEMME/Twese Hamwe

ACKNOWLEDGMENTS

The editors are extremely grateful for the financial support provided by the Cooperative for Assistance and Relief (CARE–UK) and the United Nations, without which the publication of this book would not have been possible. We are also grateful to OXFAM and Save the Children–UK, which helped to finance the "Genocide: A Collective Memory" seminar. In particular, we would like to thank Rowland Roome of CARE–Rwanda, Robert Maletta of OXFAM, Randolph Kent and Charles Petrie of the United Nations Rwanda Emergency Operation (UNREO), and Alain Sigg of the International Criminal Tribunal for Rwanda; their support was instrumental in making the seminar a success. We are also very grateful to Charles Dambach of the National Peace Corps Association for his support and for believing in this project from the outset, and to Laurie Harper of the Sebastian Agency for believing in this book.

In addition, we would like to acknowledge the invaluable contributions of Jennifer Milligan and Katherine Berry to the translation and editing of this book, and the support provided by Ambassador and Mrs.

David Rawson and the staff of the U.S. embassy and U.S. Information Service in Kigali.

Our deepest thanks are owed to the speakers at the seminar, both Rwandans and members of the international community, who came to share their experiences and their views with us. We would also like to thank those who contributed to the planning and organization of the seminar and who participated in the lively discussions that it provoked.

Finally, we would like to thank our parents and our families who have been unconditionally supportive since our evacuation and throughout the process of writing this book.

CHRONOLOGY

1885

In negotiations between the European powers, Rwanda is given to the Germans as part of their empire at the Conference of Berlin.

1894

The first German explorer, Count von Gotzen, arrives in Rwanda.

1895

Mwami Kigeri Rwabugiri dies and is succeeded by *Mwami* Mibambwe Rutarindwa.

1896

Mwami Rutarindwa is assassinated at Rucunshu. The young *Mwami* Yuhi Musinga is crowned.

1899

Ruanda-Urundi is incorporated into German East Africa and Germany establishes colonial rule.

1900

The White Fathers establish their first mission in Rwanda.

1907

Germany opens a diplomatic residence and assigns a military commander to Rwanda.

1911

Northern Hutu chiefs, angry over their loss of political autonomy to the *mwami* under German colonial rule, stage an uprising. The uprising is suppressed by German troops and Tutsi chiefs, leaving enduring bitterness among northern Hutus.

1916

Anglo-Belgian troops defeat the Germans at Shagni.

1926

The League of Nations gives Belgium trusteeship over Rwanda.

1930

The Belgians create an administrative structure based on ethnic discrimination, consolidating their power through the Tutsi chiefs. By implementing forced labor policies through the Tutsis, the Belgians make them the primary target for the resentment of the local population.

1931

Mwami Musinga is deposed by the Belgians and replaced by his son, Charles Rudahigwa Mutara, who is more susceptible to the influence of the colonialists and the Church. Tutsis are named to head all chieftancies, effectively spreading their power across the entire country.

1933

The Belgians introduce identity cards that classify all Rwandans into ethnic groups.

1945

The United Nations gives Belgium trusteeship over Rwanda with the mission of moving Rwanda toward independence.

1952

Belgium appoints the first representative councils.

1957

The *Bahutu Manifesto*, criticizing the Tutsi monopoly and calling for Hutu emancipation from the Tutsis and the Belgians, is written by a group of Hutu intellectuals and supported by the Catholic Church. The Party for the Emancipation of the Hutu (PARMEHUTU) is formed.

1959

Mwami Rudahigwa dies mysteriously in Bujumbura while under the care of a Belgian doctor. He is succeeded by his brother, Kigeri Ndahindurwa. The Hutu "social revolution" begins with a peasant revolt, supported by the Belgians, that leaves 20,000 Tutsis dead and results in a mass exodus of Tutsis, mainly into Uganda.

1960

The PARMEHUTU win an overwhelming victory in Rwanda's first municipal elections, organized by Belgian colonial rulers. *Mwami* Kigeri Ndahindurwa decides to remain in the Congo, following independence celebrations there.

1961

A republic is proclaimed by the PARMEHUTU and the monarchy is abolished by referendum. The first parliamentary elections are held on 25 September. The PARMEHUTU wins 78 percent of the vote.

1962

Rwanda and Burundi become officially independent from Belgium. Gregoire Kayibanda, a PARMEHUTU party member, is elected first president of the Rwandan First Republic.

1959–1963

Repeated attacks force more than 200,000 Tutsis into exile in neighboring countries.

1963

In December, small groups of Tutsi refugees from Burundi (commonly referred to as *Inyenzi*) stage minor attacks across the border into

Rwanda, deepening ethnic tension and provoking massive reprisals against the Tutsis still in Rwanda. Upwards of 1,000 Tutsis are killed, sending a new wave of Tutsi refugees to neighboring Uganda, Burundi, Zaire, and Tanzania. By the mid-1960s, half of the Tutsi population lives outside the borders of Rwanda.

1967

Continued cross-border attacks by Tutsi exiles provoke further anti-Tutsi pogroms in Rwanda.

1973

Renewed anti-Tutsi persecution is organized by the government; Tutsis are purged from universities. The army chief of staff, General Juvenal Habyarimana, seizes power, overthrowing President Kayibanda in a July 1973 coup d'état. Habyarimana's government institutes a policy of ethnic quotas in all public service employment, restricting Tutsis to 9 percent of available jobs. Kayibanda and other leaders of the First Republic are imprisoned, and many die under mysterious circumstances.

1975

Habyarimana founds a new party, the National Revolutionary Movement for Development (*Mouvement Révolutionnaire National pour le Développement*, or MRND.) The Second Republic begins.

Hutus are given preference in public service and military jobs, with further preference going to Hutus from the president's home area of northern Rwanda. These policies of Tutsi exclusion remain in force until 1990.

1978

A new constitution declares MRND to be Rwanda's only party. Habyarimana is reelected, with more than 99 percent of the vote.

1979

The National Rwandan Union is created in Kenya.

1983

President Habyarimana is again reelected, with a 99 percent plurality.

1986

Rwandan exiles fight with Yoweri Museveni's National Resistance Army (NRA), seizing power and overthrowing the violent dictatorial regime of Milton Obote in Uganda. The National Rwandan Union is renamed the Rwandan Patriotic Front (RPF).

1988

Once more, Habyarimana wins reelection with a 99 percent majority.

1989

The bottom falls out of the coffee market, leaving Rwanda in a severe economic depression.

1990–1991

Civilian militias known as *Interahamwe* are armed and trained by the Rwandan army throughout the country. President Habyarimana gives lip service to Western donors about establishing a genuine multiparty system with power sharing, while he stalls and sabotages these efforts and persecutes opposition politicians and the media. Thousands of Tutsis are killed in massacres throughout the country.

From 1990 on, the sheer number of incidents requires a month-by-month, even day-by-day, breakdown.

July 1990

Giving in to pressure from Western aid donors, Habyarimana agrees to separate the MRND party from the state and to establish a multiparty democracy. Negotiations among Rwanda, Uganda, and the United Nations High Commission on Refugees (UNHCR) on the repatriation of Rwandan refugees continue.

October 1990

The RPF attacks Rwanda from Uganda on 1 October, demanding the right to resettle thousands of refugees and political reforms that include the establishment of a multiparty system in Rwanda. Belgian and French forces intervene to evacuate their citizens and prop up the government. RPF troops are stopped before they reach Kigali, largely by French and Belgian intervention. The RPF falls back to the north and a guerilla war begins. Belgium withdraws its troops, but French troops remain to support the Rwandan army. Massive arrests of up to 10,000 Tutsis and political opponents are made in reprisal. The Rwandan army massacres between 500 and 1,000 Tutsis at Mutura, and 400 Tutsis at Kibirira.

November 1990

Negotiations in Goma, Zaire, produce a cease-fire. Rwanda also agrees to allow an observer force from the Organization of African Unity (OAU).

Habyarimana introduces a multiparty system and announces the abolition of ethnic identity cards. (Identity cards, however, are never abolished.)

January 1991

The RPF attacks again from the north of the country. Ruhengeri prison is liberated by RPF troops. The massacre of 500 to 1,000 Bagogwe Tutsis near Ruhengeri begins. Trials of arrested RPF "collaborators" start, resulting in several death sentences.

March 1991

The Rwandan government reaches a cease-fire with the RPF, including an agreement to integrate it in a transitional government.

June 1991

The Rwandan constitution is modified to allow multiparty democracy and freedom of the press.

July 1991

Opposition parties are formed, including the Democratic Republican Movement (MDR), the Liberal Party (PL), the Social-Democratic Party (PSD), and the Christian-Democratic Party (PDC).

November 1991

Widespread violence erupts against the Tutsis throughout Rwanda.

March 1992

At least 300 Tutsis are massacred at Bugesera. The Hutu extremist party, the Coalition for the Defense of the Republic (CDR), is formed. CDR and MRND create militias of their extremist Hutu supporters.

May 1992

A new offensive by the RPF in the north of the country creates a massive displacement of the population. MRND militias violently attack civilians.

July 1992

The RPF and the government of Rwanda sign a cease-fire in Arusha, Tanzania.

August 1992

The peace conference formally opens on 10 August in Arusha, Tanzania. Militias massacre large numbers of Tutsis in the Kibuye region of Rwanda.

October 1992

More violent demonstrations by MRND and CDR militias take place.

November 1992

Dr. Leon Mugesera, a prominent Hutu activist, calls for Hutus to "send the Tutsis back to Ethiopia" via the rivers of Rwanda. Extremist Hutu *Interahamwe* respond with an escalation in political violence. Despite government attempts to stop it, a demonstration in favor of the peace talks and against Habyarimana's veto takes place

December 1992

In Arusha, Habyarimana refuses to sign a protocol on power sharing and a transitional parliament. In Rwanda, massacres of Tutsis and Hutu opposition members occur in the Gisenyi region.

January 1993

The protocol of the Arusha Peace Accords calls for a transitional government, to include opposition parties and the RPF. Habyarimana does not attend the signing. Militias continue to provoke violence and unrest throughout Rwanda. Some 300 people are killed in organized massacres in the northwestern region of Rwanda. The International Commission of Inquiry on Human Rights Violations Since 1 October 1990 visits Rwanda.

February 1993

The RPF launches a new offensive, occupying the important prefectures of Ruhengeri and Byumba, and threatening to take Kigali. France sends 300 additional troops and weapons to stop the offensive. One million people flee in front of advancing RPF troops. Negotiations on the withdrawal of French troops and their replacement with United Nations peacekeepers or OAU troops begin between the RPF and the opposition parties within the government.

March 1993

A new cease-fire is negotiated in Dar-es-Salaam between the Rwandan government and the RPF. The RPF withdraws to the north. The United Nations Security Council adopts Resolution 812, authorizing an intervention force in Rwanda. The 300 French reinforcement troops are withdrawn.

The International Commission of Inquiry publishes its report, citing grave human rights violations that it describes as "genocide" on the part of the government. Several donor countries threaten Rwanda with sanctions as a result of the report.

May–June 1993

New accords are signed in Arusha concerning refugee repatriation and unification of the armed forces of the Rwandan government and the RPF. Emmanuel Gapyisi, leader of the MDR, is assassinated. MDR's Agathe Uwilingiyimana is named prime minister of the new transitional government.

8 July 1993

The extremist Hutu *Radio Télévision Libre des Mille Collines* (Thousand Hills Free Radio-Television) (RTLM) begins its "hate radio" broadcasting throughout Rwanda.

August 1993

The RPF and Habyarimana sign the comprehensive version of the Arusha Peace Accords. These include provisions for the installation of a transitional government including the RPF, the unification of the armies, demobilization, and the arrival of the United Nations Assistance Mission to Rwanda (UNAMIR).

October 1993

The United Nations Security Council approves Resolution 872, creating UNAMIR, a force of 2,500 soldiers from 23 countries. In two days in mid-October, 37 MRND supporters are murdered in the region of Ruhengeri.

November–December 1993

The French troops leave Rwanda; UNAMIR troops are deployed. Six hundred RPF troops arrive in Kigali on 28 December as part of the Arusha Peace Accords.

January 1994

President Habyarimana takes the oath of office according to the provisions of the Arusha Peace Accords. The swearing-in of the rest of the transitional government is repeatedly blocked by the president and his "Hutu Power" allies.

February 1994

Two well-known political leaders, Felicien Gatabazi of the PSD and Martin Bucyana of the extremist group CDR, are assassinated within days of each other. The perpetrators are neither identified nor punished. Violence escalates in Kigali and around the country.

6 April 1994

Returning from a summit meeting at Dar-es-Salaam, the plane carrying the presidents of Rwanda and Burundi, Juvenal Habyarimana and Cyprien Ntaryamira, is shot down on its approach to the Kigali airport. The perpetrators remain unknown to this day. Within moments of the crash, systematic and widespread massacres of opposition leaders of the PSD, MDR, and PL begin. Military and militia roadblocks go up all over Kigali. Violence escalates, targeting Tutsis, Hutu opposition members, and moderates.

7 April 1994

Prime Minister Uwilingiyimana is tortured, mutilated, and assassinated by soldiers of the Rwandan army. The Presidential Guard disarms the 10 Belgian UNAMIR soldiers guarding the prime minister, then systematically tortures and murders them.

RPF troops in Kigali leave their garrison. Coordinated and extensive massacres are carried out by the Rwandan army and militia groups in Kigali and in the countryside.

8 April 1994

The RPF launches an offensive in the north. Theodore Sindikubwabo, former speaker of parliament, announces the formation of an interim government and declares himself interim president. Jean Kambanda of the MDR is named prime minister.

9 April 1994

French and Belgian paratroopers assist with the evacuation of expatriates. Belgium withdraws its entire force.

11 April 1994

The Red Cross and other relief organizations estimate that 20,000 people have been killed in Kigali between 6 and 11 April. Foreign journalists are prohibited from entering the country by the interim government.

12 April 1994

RPF reinforcements reach Kigali; the battle of Kigali begins. The interim government moves from Kigali to Gitarama. The massacre of Tutsis continues throughout Rwanda.

19 April 1994

Massacres begin in Butare, which had previously been spared the worst of the violence. The prefect of Butare, who had opposed the massacres, is arrested and killed with his whole family. A hard-line extremist takes his place.

21 April 1994

The UN Security Council passes Resolution 912 to redefine UNAMIR's mandate and reduce the number of UN troops and observers from 2,500 to 270. The mandate remains unchanged, leaving troops unable to use weapons.

30 April 1994

The United Nations High Commission for Refugees (UNHCR) reports the largest known mass refugee exodus, when an estimated 250,000 people flee across the Rwandan border to Tanzania. The Security Council affirms the need to protect the refugees and to help restore order in Rwanda. The affirmation, which also condemns the killing, omits the word "genocide," leaving the United Nations without responsibility to prevent the violence and punish the perpetrators. There is no mention of the peacekeeping force or the revision of its mandate. Relief organizations estimate that at least 150,000 people have been killed since 6 April, and another 1.3 million displaced.

17 May 1994

The Security Council votes on Resolution 918, demanding a cease-fire in Rwanda and an end to the massacres, imposing an arms embargo on both parties, and authorizing the deployment of 5,500 United Nations troops (UNAMIR II).

The U.S. State Department holds a press conference and says that "acts of genocide may have occurred" in Rwanda.

22 May 1994

The RPF captures the Kigali airport and the Kanombe barracks, and extends its control in the northern and eastern regions.

25 May 1994

The United Nations High Commissioner for Human Rights sends René Degni-Segui to investigate grave violations of international human rights law in Rwanda.

27 May 1994

UN forces evacuate the first refugees from the Mille Collines Hotel.

8 June 1994

The RPF announces that three bishops and 10 priests have been killed by RPF soldiers.

10 June 1994

One hundred seventy Tutsis are massacred in Saint André Church in Kigali.

17 June 1994

France informs the UN Security Council that it will intervene in Rwanda by sending 2,500 troops as an interim peacekeeping force until UNAMIR troops arrive.

22 June 1994

The Security Council narrowly passes Resolution 929, authorizing armed humanitarian intervention in Rwanda, at the request of the French. The French receive approval for *Opération Turquoise* and are given the right to deploy armed French soldiers under a UN peace-keeping mandate.

23 June 1994

French troops arrive in Rwanda as part of *Opération Turquoise*.

28 June 1994

A report issued by the special investigator of the United Nations Commission on Human Rights states that the murder of the Tutsis in Rwanda is an organized and systematic campaign of genocide and calls for an international tribunal to bring the organizers of the genocide to justice.

1 July 1994

The UN Security Council votes on Resolution 935, which calls for a commission of experts to examine evidence of "possible acts of genocide."

4 July 1994

Kigali and Butare are captured by the RPF. Its leadership states its intention to establish a coalition government based upon the frame-work in the Arusha Peace Accords. France creates a "safe humanitarian zone," the *Zone Turquoise*, in the southwest prefectures of Gikongoro, Cyangugu, and Kibuye. The French government orders its troops to stop the RPF advance.

13 July 1994

The RPF takes Ruhengeri in northern Rwanda, prompting an exodus of Rwandans toward Goma, Zaire. Approximately 12,000 refugees per hour cross the border.

15 July 1994

The U.S. government withdraws its recognition of the former government of Rwanda. Members of the interim government escape to the *Zone Turquoise* and are protected by French troops.

17 July 1994

The RPF takes the last government stronghold, in Gisenyi, and declares an end to the war.

19 July 1994

A government of national unity is formed in Kigali, and Pasteur Bizimungu and Faustin Twagiramungu are sworn in as president and prime minister, respectively. Members of the MRND and CDR are excluded from the new government. RPF commander Major-General Paul Kagame is appointed minister of defense and vice president. Cholera is diagnosed among refugees in Goma.

22 July 1994

The U.S. government announces a massive relief operation for Rwanda.

28 July 1994

The secretary general of the United Nations announces the creation of the International Commission of Inquiry to identify those responsible for acts of genocide committed in Rwanda. The UN Security Council finally reaches an agreement, resolving to send an international force to Rwanda.

29 July 1994

France begins the withdrawal of its *Opération Turquoise* troops.

31 July 1994

As part of Operation Support Hope, the first contingent of the U.S. military arrives in Kigali to deliver humanitarian assistance.

24 August 1994

The last *Opération Turquoise* troops depart; UNAMIR forces take over operations.

Major refugee movements occur toward the south of Rwanda and into Bukavu, Zaire.

29 August 1994

The new government of Rwanda agrees to allow trials before an international tribunal to be established by the UN Security Council.

8 November 1994

United Nations Security Council Resolution 955 is adopted, establishing an international court for Rwandan war criminals.

24 December 1994

Hutu refugees announce the establishment of a government-in-exile in the refugee camps in Zaire.

6 April 1995

A memorial service for the victims of the genocide is held in Kigali. Silent and peaceful demonstrations occur throughout Rwanda. A mass grave discovered behind the *Centre Hospitalier de Kigali* (Kigali Hospital Center) is estimated to contain 5,000 to 6,000 genocide victims.

22 April 1995

Soldiers of the RPF massacre internally displaced persons (IDP) in the Kibeho IDP camp. Conflicting reports of the number of dead are released by the government and relief organizations. Refugees are forced from IDP camps throughout the country and expected to return to their home districts.

May 1995

Tension increases between the United Nations and the Rwandan government, since the international criminal tribunal has not indicted a single war criminal, and aid to Rwanda is not forthcoming. The Rwandan government announces that peacekeepers were deployed too late to stop the genocide and that there is no longer any need for a peacekeeping effort.

10 June 1995

The UN Security Council unanimously agrees to cut the number of peacekeeping troops in Rwanda by more than half, after repeated requests from the Rwandan government.

23–26 August 1995

Mobutu Sese Seko, president of Zaire, announces his intention to expel refugees from the camps in Goma and threatens to force the repatriation of all refugees on Zairian soil.

28 August 1995

Hutu Prime Minister Faustin Twagiramungu resigns and is replaced three days later by Pierre-Céléstin Rwigyema.

23 November 1995

Judge Richard Goldstone, the prosecutor of the International Court for War Criminals of Rwanda, issues his first indictment.

12 December 1995

The International Criminal Tribunal for Rwanda announces indictments against eight suspects, charging them with crimes against humanity and genocide.

13 December 1995

UNAMIR's mandate in Rwanda is extended for three months by United Nations Security Council Resolution 1019. The resolution reduces the number of troops from 2,100 to 1,400 and refocuses their activities on the return of Rwandan refugees.

October 1996

The number of genocide suspects in Rwandan jails surpasses 92,000. Kigali Central Prison, designed to hold 2,000 people, holds more than 8,000 prisoners. New arrests average 600 per week.

November 1996

Massive repatriation of refugees from Zaire occurs as fighting between the rebel Force for the Liberation of Congo/Zaire (led by Laurent Kabila) and the Zairian Armed Forces (FAZ) accelerates. The Rwandan government issues a moratorium on arrests of suspected genocide perpetrators.

December 1996

In Rwanda national trials of those accused of organizing and participating in the 1994 genocide begin.

17 December 1996

The Tanzanian government closes the refugee camps within its borders and repatriates the refugees. Hutu militia activity is still strong within the camps, and many refugees are killed when they try to return to Rwanda.

8 March 1996

UNAMIR begins to pull out its remaining 1,400 troops after Rwandan officials refuse to allow extension of their mandate. Their withdrawal is met with anti-UN demonstrations by survivor groups.

12 March 1996

"Lessons from the Rwanda Experience," a major evaluation report sponsored by 20 donor nations, is issued. The report criticizes the role of the UN, France, the United States, and the media.

10 January 1997

Jean Paul Akayesu, accused of ordering mass killings in his area and organizing troops, is the first case to come before the international criminal tribunal for Rwanda. The trial is held in Arusha, Tanzania.

January 1997

National trials continue in Rwanda. Peogratis Bizimana is the first suspect to be sentenced to death for his role in the genocide. A woman who testified against Jean Paul Akayesu at the International Criminal Tribunal is murdered, along with her husband and seven children. An extremist group of Hutus is suspected in the murders.

2 February 1997

As widely attended local trials of suspects in the genocide begin in their home villages, the UN Human Rights Field Operation for Rwanda issues a brief expressing "serious concern" about the suspects' ability to receive a fair trial, the lack of qualified lawyers, and the general disinterest in defending accused participants in the genocide. Guy Pinard, a Canadian priest who witnessed the genocide, is murdered while saying mass.

5 February 1997

In Cyangugu, five UN human rights field officers are murdered by suspected Hutu extremists. The UN Center for Human Rights responds by removing all field officers from the region. Several aid agencies issue reports openly criticizing the management of the international criminal tribunal.

26 February 1997

UN Secretary General Kofi Annan fires chief administrator Andronico Adede and deputy prosecutor Honore Rakoromoanana of the International Criminal Tribunal for Rwanda, citing ineffective and poor management. A Nigerian, Agwu Okali, is appointed as the new chief administrator. The court has indicted only 23 suspects by the date of this change in personnel.

16 May 1997

As one of his last acts as head of state of the former Zaire (now Republic of Congo), President Mobutu Sese Seko orders the cremation of the body of Rwanda's former president Juvenal Habyarimana. Habyarimana's corpse was secretly brought to the capital, Kinshasa, from Mobutu's northern hometown of Gbadolite, where it had been kept in a private mausoleum built by Mobutu especially for Habyarimana. It is unclear how Mobutu obtained the body.

EDITORS' NOTES

The text of this book is based on translated transcripts from the conference "Genocide: A Collective Memory," which took place in Kigali, Rwanda, on 19 and 20 January 1995. Both the conference and this book were intended primarily to offer Rwandans the opportunity to speak about the horrible experience their country had just been through and to raise awareness among non-Rwandans about the origins and impact of the genocide.

The idea for this conference was developed in collaboration with a number of individuals, in particular Charles Petrie of UNREO. Petrie arrived in Rwanda during the genocide and expressed concern that many of the newly arrived foreign relief workers did not fully appreciate the complex context of postgenocide reconstruction efforts.

Interested individuals were invited to contribute to the planning and organization of the conference, and through a participatory process it developed into something more meaningful than a simple background briefing for international workers. Over the course of the planning meetings, it became obvious that this conference should be as much (if not more) about Rwandans discussing their experiences and sharing their opinions on Rwanda's past, on the genocide, and on the future of their country as it was about improving outsiders' understanding of Rwanda. Above all, we realized, it was a conference about remembering.

To improve the flow of the book, the order of the text varies slightly from that of the conference presentations. During the course of the conference, speakers often made comments or asked questions in response to the information being presented. Because these comments were not part of formal presentations, they are untitled and are identified only by the name and organization of the speaker. Due to technical difficulties with recording equipment, some presentations made at the conference are not included in this book. In addition, not all of the comments made during question-and-answer periods have been included. After the conference, some of the speakers provided the editors with additional written material to complement their presentations. The material included in Chapter 4, "The Voice of Extremism," was translated specifically for this book and was not presented at the conference.

As translators and editors, we have made a concerted effort to remain as faithful as possible to the words of the speakers at the conference "Genocide: A Collective Memory." Although as individuals we share many of the beliefs and concerns of our Rwandan colleagues, their words and opinions are their own.

INTRODUCTION: COLLECTING MEMORY

■ JOHN A. BERRY AND CAROL POTT BERRY

When we were evacuated from Rwanda on 9 April 1994, there were many people to whom we were unable to say good-bye. When we returned six months later, most of them were either buried in mass graves or had fled Rwanda. Our return, the "Genocide: A Collective Memory" conference, and this book are in many ways an effort to say good-bye not only to our friends and colleagues, but also to the hundreds of thousands of other Rwandans we will never have the chance to know and to a period in Rwandan history that we hope will never be repeated.

What happened in Rwanda has much more important implications than those of our individual memories. Broadcast live around the world, the genocide in Rwanda revealed a very deep, very basic failure in humanity—a failure on the part of the former government of Rwanda and the population that, willingly or by force, committed genocide, and a failure on the part of the international community that refused to understand the events in Rwanda until it was too late and then retreated in the face of genocide. This book and the conference from which it originated attempt to understand the impact of this massive human failure through the words of the people who experienced it.

In organizing the conference we made an effort to be both balanced and integrated in our approach. We pursued balance by including speakers from a range of different backgrounds with a variety of points of view on the situation in Rwanda. They included academics, journalists, human-rights activists, government officials, army officers, ordinary Rwandan men and women, and members of the international community who were in Rwanda during the genocide. Although for obvious reasons we were not able to invite representatives from the former government to the conference, we have attempted to present their perspective in this book through a translation of "*Le Peuple Rwandais Accuse . . . ,*"[1] an open letter to the international community written by members of the former interim government.

We sought to integrate the presentations at the conference by including speakers from a range of disciplines with different approaches to understanding what happened in Rwanda. These approaches included witness testimony and historical, political, social, cultural, demographic, and legal perspectives on the genocide. This multidisciplinary approach allowed the speakers to explore issues and answer questions from a variety of different angles.

Despite this variety of speakers and approaches, there were a few questions that almost every presentation addressed: What led to the genocide? What was the genocide? What are the implications of the genocide for the future of Rwanda?

Factors Leading to the Genocide

The speakers at the conference attributed different levels of significance to the factors that led Rwanda into violence, but most agreed on the origins of the genocide. Major factors cited as playing a part in the genocide include the lack of justice in crimes against the Tutsis, control of political power, racism, hatred, fear, and ignorance.

Although these factors influenced each other or acted in synergy, the one component mentioned most often was the "culture of impunity." For 35 years, no one on a governmental or individual level was held accountable for the systematic murder of Tutsis. Each unpunished massacre added to the inequity of the previous one. The culture of impunity that this created eventually culminated in genocide.

During the genocide, some members of the international community continued to refer to the situation in Rwanda as yet another case, though certainly worse than others, of African tribal violence. This simplification was not only naive and uninformed, but was also a gross misconception of what was actually happening in Rwanda. Genocide is an inherently political act, manifested in the effort to exterminate an entire racial group. In essence, the genocide in Rwanda had as much to do with tribalism as the Holocaust did in Europe. Both were organized and implemented by a small group of extremist politicians using every means possible to hold power. Unaccountable before the law, this small group of individuals transformed racial extremism, oppression, and violence into legitimate means of exercising political authority.

For the leaders of the First and Second Republics[2] in Rwanda, as for the leaders of the Third Reich in Germany, the incitement of racial hatred was a deliberate political technique used to rally their supporters and distract attention from the real domestic problems of the country.[3]

The leaders of the First and Second Republics used two very effective mechanisms to manipulate and mobilize popular opinion against the Tutsis: hatred and fear. With the support of members of the Rwandan intellectual elite, Hutu extremists propagated a revisionist history of relations between the Hutus and the Tutsis that were not based on cohabitation and exchange but rather on segregation and violence. This myth was so successful that on the eve of independence, Hutu politicians rallied the people to throw out the "feudal colonialists," referring not to the Belgians who had ruled Rwanda for 40 years, but to the Tutsis with whom the Hutus had lived side by side for 400 years.

Using this same hatred and the threat of a military invasion by the Rwandan Patriotic Front (RPF), the leaders of the First and Second Republics instilled an exaggerated sense of fear in the population, to the point that many people were convinced that if an invasion occurred they would be mutilated, killed, or even eaten alive by Tutsi soldiers.[4] In the dark days of the genocide, the government and its militias also used fear to mobilize the population to commit genocide—to kill or be killed.

The last factor leading to the genocide—the use of ignorance and the control of information—applies to the government's approach both to its own people and to the international community. In many ways, the people of Rwanda were kept in the dark about events inside and outside of Rwanda that ultimately made it easier to manipulate popular opinion through extremist newspapers and radio. For close to 35 years, the international community remained almost willfully ignorant of the significance of the myriad abuses, large and small, that eventually led to the genocide in Rwanda. This was due in part to the government's ability to play on donors' ignorance by telling them what they wanted to hear, and in part to the international community's ability to ignore sporadic massacres, the arming and training of militias, hate-radio broadcasts, and regular reports on government abuses from human-rights organizations.

Whether a genocide in Rwanda was inevitable, given the above factors, is debatable. It cannot, however, be argued that no one knew what was happening in Rwanda, or that there was nothing that could have been done to stop the genocide. The elaborate deception of the Rwandan people by the leaders of the First and Second Republics lasted for more than three decades,[5] but its brutality was clear from the beginning. It was clear that the former government considered persecution of the Tutsis as the necessary price of Hutu emancipation. It was also clear from the beginning that the international community had an important influence over events in Rwanda, an influence that it chose to exercise only sporadically.

Understanding the Genocide in Rwanda

For an event that was so widely covered by the media, the genocide in Rwanda largely remains misunderstood by the international community. While the former allied powers celebrated the 50th anniversary of the Normandy invasion that eventually brought an end to the Holocaust in Europe, another genocide was taking place in Africa— another genocide that members of the international community, if they had demonstrated the unity that led to victory in Europe, could have acted to stop.

However distracted and fractious the international community is today, it is crucial to emphasize that genocide is something that concerns all of humanity. The implications of genocide are so vast and so horrible that they invoke a moral responsibility not only on the part of the international community and its member states, but on the part of humanity and all of the individuals who comprise it. The obligation to oppose genocide should know no boundaries. Even if genocide takes place in a small country in the middle of Africa such as Rwanda, it still concerns all of humanity, and humanity—represented by individuals, states, and the international community—has a duty to intervene.

There are many important misconceptions about what happened in Rwanda from April to July 1994. Some people still believe that what took place was not actually a genocide of the Tutsis, or that it was a double genocide of both Hutus and Tutsis, or, as the former government alleges, that it was a genocide of Hutus by Tutsis. Yet as the speakers at the "Collective Memory" conference made very clear, it was a genocide. This was neither a series of politically inspired massacres, nor an "African tribal conflict," nor the result of ethnic division, demographic pressures, or increasing poverty (although these could be considered as contributing factors). It was genocide. Certainly members of the opposition were killed for their political beliefs, but at the heart of what happened in Rwanda is the fact that Tutsis were killed for having been born.

Understanding the genocide in Rwanda also requires comprehending the amazing extent to which it was planned in advance. Under the gaze of the international community, the former government of Rwanda prepared and executed a genocide that was organized in minute detail. Unlike the Nazi genocide that was carried out in industrial gas chambers by specially selected soldiers at isolated concentration camps, the Rwandan genocide was mainly executed with agricultural tools, involved all socioeconomic groups, and took place throughout the country in full and immediate view of the public.

Finally, the genocide would not have been possible without the passive (and in some cases active) involvement of the international community. Although in the eyes of the Western public the genocide in Rwanda may have seemed to be an event that came from nowhere and flashed across television screens only to disappear as quickly as it appeared, it was, in fact, a long time in preparation.

Indeed, the West influenced events in Rwanda far more than many realize. Although Western influence in Rwanda began with the Germans at the turn of the century, it was the Belgians who played a

decisive role by imposing European racial stereotypes, supporting the
Tutsis to the detriment of the Hutus, and then shifting the blame for
colonial oppression to the Tutsis and leaving them to their fate.
Although a large number of donor countries continued to tolerate the
blatant racism of the postindependence governments of Rwanda, it was
the French who, in the name of *la francophonie*, armed and trained the
soldiers and the militias that committed the genocide. Finally, the U.S.
government has been strongly criticized by both sides of the conflict for
failing to lead the international community in a concerted and forceful
response to the genocide. While hundreds of thousands of Rwandans
were being systematically butchered, the U.S. government's reaction
was to say that "acts of genocide may have occurred."

The Implications of the Genocide

One of the most thought-provoking discussions that took place at the
"Collective Memory" conference concerned the genocide's implications
for the future of Rwanda. Despite lengthy discussions on the role of the
international community before, during, and after the genocide, the
speakers in general agreed that they, the Rwandans, must come to grips
with what their compatriots have brought upon their country. It was
Rwandans who planned, organized, and executed the genocide. It was
Rwandans who were its victims, and it is Rwandans who must find
ways to cope with its effects. The international community has a
responsibility to support the Rwandan people in this effort, but in the
end it will be up to Rwanda to rebuild the nation and rehabilitate its
people after the genocide.

The reconstruction of Rwanda will not take place without some
form of reconciliation, and reconciliation cannot take place without
justice. Neither the people of Rwanda nor the international community
can remain neutral in the face of genocide. We all need to recognize
that what has taken place is a crime against humanity that must be
investigated, tried, and punished. Justice must be done and Rwandans
(both inside the country and outside, in the refugee camps) must be
able to witness it.

The end of the last genocide trial should not be misconstrued as the
end of the genocide. It is not an exaggeration to say that Rwanda's
genocide changed the world, and both Rwandans and members of the
international community have an obligation to reflect on the implica-

tions of these changes. Rwandans must reexamine their perception of themselves and their role in the future of the country. The international community must reexamine its understanding of Rwanda and its role there. The international community must also consider how it will react to genocide if and when it occurs again. The question was asked several times: If the genocide in Rwanda was not sufficiently horrific to provoke a timely response, then what level of inhumanity will it take to move the international community to action?

In addition, donor governments must ask themselves how they could continue, knowingly or unknowingly, to provide aid to a government that practiced racism and instituted segregationalist policies, while carefully preparing a genocide. The donor community must be aware that even humanitarian assistance has political implications, and that in supporting a blatantly racist and oppressive regime it undermines not only the positive impact of the assistance it provides but also its own moral standing.

One cannot escape the ironic fact that the genocide in Rwanda took place 50 years after the Holocaust, and that the United Nations—the organization that was created in part to ensure that genocide would never happen again—did not attempt to stop it. Another irony was the fact that the celebrations for the 50th anniversary of the liberation of Auschwitz and the "Genocide: A Collective Memory" conference took place on the same day. As the world was mourning the victims of the Holocaust, we were listening to survivor testimony about the Rwandan genocide.

The parallels between the Holocaust and the Rwandan genocide are too numerous to recount here, but one of the crucial differences is that the international community had a much greater ability to know what was taking place in Rwanda—it was broadcast around the world on Cable News Network (CNN)—and a much greater ability to stop it (the military strength of Rwanda and Hitler's Germany are not comparable). After the Holocaust, the world told itself that "never again" would it allow genocide to take place. In Rwanda, "never again" happened again.

As editors, we do not believe that this book can alone keep a promise that the former government of Rwanda and the international community decided not to keep. At the same time, in a world of headlines instantly created and instantly forgotten, we feel it is vital that the genocide in Rwanda be remembered. The effort must be a collective one. For the sake of humanity, we cannot afford to forget.

Notes

1. "The Rwandan People Accuse . . . ," the "open letter" written from Zaire by the minister of information of the interim government, responds to accusations of involvement in the genocide. A full translation is found in Chapter 4.

2. "First Republic" refers to the period in Rwanda governed by the Gregoire Kayibanda regime, "Second Republic" to the Juvenal Habyarimana regime. Both the First and Second Republics are further explained in Chapter 2.

3. The editors use the word "racial" in this case because it has been argued that Hutus and Tutsis share the same language, culture, history, and religion and therefore are members of the same ethnic group.

4. The myth of the "evil Tutsi soldiers of the RPF" is further explained in Chapter 2. Rwandan Patriotic Front soldiers, nicknamed the *Inkotanyi* (Kinyarwanda for "fierce fighters"), were renowned for their talents on the battlefield and mythologized as cannibals and kidnappers.

5. The First Republic lasted from 1961 through 1973. It was overthrown by the leaders of the Second Republic, which lasted from 1973 through 1994.

PERSPECTIVES ON THE GENOCIDE IN RWANDA

Introduction

JOHN A. BERRY AND CAROL POTT BERRY

It is difficult to describe the atmosphere in which the following testimony was given. This portion of the conference was held at the U.S. embassy's U.S. Information Service auditorium in Kigali on 19 January 1995. The auditorium posted a capacity of 75 people, yet more than a hundred—mainly expatriate employees of international nongovernmental organizations (NGOs)—squeezed in to hear the testimony that follows.

Most of the members of the international community who attended the conference arrived in Rwanda after the genocide. They came to the conference to listen to Rwandans talk about their personal experiences during the genocide and to try to reach a better understanding of what had happened in Rwanda from April to July 1994. The Rwandans who gave testimony came to share their intimate, complex, and difficult experiences with a room full of foreigners, most of whom they had never met. These same foreigners represented the international community that only six months before had stood by and watched while genocidal massacres raged across Rwanda.

As members of that same international community, we were struck by several things during the course of the conference. The first was the extent to which the genocide affected the entire population of Rwanda. Everyone alive in Rwanda has a story to tell about the genocide. The conference provided participants with an opportunity to reflect on the human impact of the genocide on the people of Rwanda. Although it is often talked about in terms of numbers ranging from 500,000 to more than a million dead, at its heart the genocide was not about numbers but about people—individuals killing and being killed. The testimony and discussions that took place at the conference forced those who attended to realize the importance of a forum where the people of Rwanda can relate their experiences and the international community can listen.

In choosing speakers to present testimony at the conference, we made an effort to invite individuals from all walks of life, with a wide range of experiences and perspectives. This group included current and former members of the Rwandan government, journalists, and representatives from nongovernmental and women's organizations. Although each of the speakers had a different experience and perspective on the genocide, all of the Rwandans who spoke were deeply and personally affected by it. The speakers offered their testimony as concerned individuals and Rwandans, not as representatives of the organizations or institutions for which they work.

As the organizers of the conference, we struggled with the fact that in inviting Rwandans to speak about their experiences during the genocide we would be asking them to bring up a deeply emotional, personal subject in a very public forum. Only after sharing this fear with Rwandan colleagues did we feel assured that no matter how difficult the stories were to recount, the international community in Rwanda needed to listen to them. During the conference, we were impressed by the calm manner in which the presenters described events that seemed inconceivable in their horror. As editors and organizers of the conference and as human beings, we deeply appreciate how difficult it was for our Rwandan colleagues to recount these very personal histories, and we are sincerely grateful to all the

Rwandans who offered their testimony at the "Collective Memory" conference.

Witness Testimony

■ ALPHONSE MARIE NKUBITO, FORMER MINISTER OF JUSTICE, GOVERNMENT OF RWANDA

I would like, for a moment, to forget the rules of diplomatic courtesy and speak simply as an individual and an advocate of human rights about what I feel, what I know, and what I lived through. What happened in Rwanda during the genocide is the past; I prefer to talk about what I would like to see happen in the future. This is not a formal statement from the Ministry of Justice, nor is it the opinion of the government of Rwanda. I have been asked to provide a perspective on the genocide and would simply like to talk about some of the things that struck me.

Months after the genocide, during the Round Table on Rwanda,[1] the international community finally decided to accept its responsibilities in the rehabilitation of Rwanda. It committed itself to helping a Rwanda that was devastated and pillaged, that had seen so much loss of life under the disinterested gaze of this same international community. All of this destruction, disorder, and looting, the massacres and the genocide—were they necessary? Why is it that the world waited for all these horrors to happen before thinking about Rwanda?

The international community in Rwanda must focus its attention on helping the Rwandans to heal their many wounds. The children of Rwanda will learn about this period in history and will ask themselves how this genocide, unequaled in history in its speed, magnitude, and thoroughness, could happen, all under the passive watch of the United Nations.

My faith in the United Nations, this honorable world organization and its institutions, has been greatly diminished by the retreat of the majority of the UNAMIR[2] forces when the massacres and the genocide were at their height. And yet, these same UNAMIR troops saw the beginning of this genocidal drama when they witnessed countless arms being unloaded by the previous regime in violation of the United Nations arms embargo. The United Nations also knew that the former government had been blocking the negotiation of the Arusha Peace Accords[3] and the reasons why it was holding up the implementation of these accords. Were there not enough indications of a pending disaster before the genocide began? Why didn't the international community react before it was too late?

Only after extensive pressure was applied by NGOs, certain governments, and international organizations, and by the secretary general of the United Nations was the decision made to reconsider the mandate of the UNAMIR forces. UNAMIR's mandate was revised and finally, after much deliberation and lost time, the number of UNAMIR soldiers was strengthened.

The current conditions in Rwanda are not the same as they were when UNAMIR was initially strengthened in the summer of 1995, and it is now time to readapt UNAMIR's mandate to this new reality. Rwanda knows the weaknesses of this well-intended organization. The procedures involved in moving the institutions of the United Nations remain extremely complicated—so complicated, in fact, that the United Nations' capacity to act quickly is greatly reduced.

After having been placed under the scrutiny of the international community, the government of Rwanda has, after a thousand and one hesitations on the part of that same community, finally begun to receive some support. The government of Rwanda encourages this support, both moral and material. This support is, in fact, necessary if the government is to succeed in its role and fulfill its duty representing the Rwandan people. Rwanda has suffered through numerous difficulties, even after the installation of the new government. There has been a resurgence of violence, in the face of which the population calls for justice.

The international community can help to assure that justice, which is needed desperately by the Rwandan people, becomes a reality. The international community cannot speak of the genocide in Rwanda without also addressing its perpetrators and the need for justice. Rwanda's situation must serve as a lesson to politicians and to the international community and force them to develop a system that can prevent crimes against humanity.

In Rwanda, we must speak strongly when we talk of the need for justice. In effect, the culture of impunity in Rwanda was the origin of repeated massacres over the course of the last 35 years. These massacres culminated in a genocide that was systematic, massive, planned in minute detail, and then broadcast by the media. The destruction of this culture of impunity by means of an effective justice system remains a priority for all Rwandans. To allow those who are guilty of genocide to go unpunished is to dishonor the memory of the innocent victims who were murdered in the name of democratic change. I am among those who believe that national reconciliation cannot proceed without the prosecution of those who planned and executed the genocide in Rwanda.

In order to prevent such crises in the future, the international community must be prepared to react forcefully to human-rights violations and to rapidly denounce those who commit such crimes. The international community will fulfill its responsibilities in Rwanda only after it has helped the country to develop its own judicial system and after the international criminal tribunal[4] is functioning. Aiding justice in Rwanda is the only way to break the vicious circle of violence. The international community can also redeem itself by helping, without conditions, in the reconstruction of Rwanda. The international community should help Rwanda by assisting in the establishment of the rule of law, promoting and monitoring human rights, helping to ensure security, and reinforcing the institutions of the country. To help Rwanda is, in the end, to help create appropriate conditions for the return of the Rwandan refugees of both yesterday and today.

The judicial system in Rwanda has been decapitated by the crisis that has shaken the country. It is sorely lacking in resources, both human and material. Rwanda calls on the international community to donate technical assistance by providing judges and investigators to deal with the enormous caseload faced by the Rwandan judicial system. The prisons of Rwanda are full to the breaking point, and yet suspected murderers continue to evade justice. After fleeing from justice, these killers have become the beneficiaries of the assistance provided by humanitarian organizations such as the Red Cross and the World Food Programme. While the innocent in Rwanda go hungry, suspected murderers and perpetrators of the genocide are fed, housed, and clothed by the international community.

▮ THOMAS KAMILINDI, JOURNALIST

I had worked at Radio Rwanda for 10 years as the French-language presenter of the news when, in March 1994, the atmosphere became unbearable, and I had to resign because I could not work under the regime in power. There are three points that I want to make quite clear. The first is the extremely barbarous nature of the events through which we all lived. The second is the extremely minute detail with which these events were prepared. The third is the distress that the Rwandan people have suffered as a result of the genocide. What I lived through, compared to what others lived through, seems banal. Imagine having to watch as people come to murder your entire family—men, women, children, and the elderly—without pity with machetes and garden tools. I again want to stress the extreme barbarity of these events. People were forced to witness this barbarism when, for example, their small children who were only a few months old had their heads smashed against a wall. The militia members would throw children in the air and see how many times they could hit them with a machete before they fell to the ground.

I saw people with their throats slit, people who had been shot, but I want to give you another shocking example of the barbarity of these crimes. This story was told to me personally by the former minister of information, Eliezer Niyitegeka, who is now with the government in exile in Zaire. He told me this at the radio station on 12 April 1994 to make me change my mind about resigning from the radio station. This story is about Prime Minister Madame Agathe Uwilingiyimana and how she died.

According to what Mr. Niyitegeka told me, two armored vehicles arrived at Prime Minister Uwilingiyimana's house with a large contingent of soldiers. The soldiers attacked her residence, and the troops that should have protected her, including the troops from UNAMIR, were overwhelmed. The prime minister hid with her family, but the government soldiers eventually found her and pulled her out from under a bed where she was trying to hide. Mr. Niyitegeka then said that the soldiers took her and her family into another room, where they told the prime minister to take her clothes off, which she did. They told her to spread her legs, which she did. The soldiers then penetrated her vagina with their bayonets in the presence of her family. They kept stabbing her until the bayonets stabbed through to her throat. They finally shot her to death in front of her whole family. Her husband and her mother were also shot, but her children managed to escape, were evacuated by UNAMIR, and are now being sheltered somewhere in Europe. I will again say that this story was meant to influence me to continue to work with these barbarians.

These are just a few examples to show you how inhuman these people were. This is the type of thing that happened to all of the important members of the opposition. All of their family members were killed. Their belongings were pillaged. What the attackers didn't want to steal they burned; then they destroyed the houses of their victims.

What happened in Rwanda was prepared in detail, well in advance. From 7 April 1994 and even on the evening of 6 April, lists of people to be killed were posted at the offices of *Radio-Télévision Libre des Mille Collines* (RTLM).[5] This I learned from people who worked there at the time. We knew the people at RTLM very well because we were colleagues; we all worked in radio. When I called them on the phone, they told me, "There is a paper that we have that lists all the people to be killed, people suspected to be accomplices of the RPF," mainly just Tutsis. My name was number two on one of these lists. These lists were well known. The houses of the people on these death lists were well known. They had been identified well in advance so that the killers almost never made a mistake in finding who they were looking for. One has to ask oneself why, even on the evening of 6 April, barricades were built immediately after the plane was shot down. Before people had time to flee, all the roads were blocked. The entire country was taken hostage by the killers.

To conclude, I would like to speak about the extremely detailed level of preparations and about RTLM, which became the real means of communication for all the killers in the country. The people at RTLM knew what was going on everywhere in the country. RTLM gave instructions about what to do to every part of the country. RTLM had the power of life and death over people by simply stating on the air that an individual should be saved or killed.

The massacres were of an incredible, almost indescribable scope. When UNAMIR pulled out, the Rwandan people were abandoned and left entirely on their own as the hostages of the killers. Even the authorities whom UNAMIR was under orders to protect were not protected. I can tell you the story of a school that the Belgians were protecting that is only eight kilometers from here. When the Belgian troops were evacuated, they left behind more than 4,000 people who had sought refuge there, among them officials whom UNAMIR had a mandate to protect. Most of these people were later killed.

When UNAMIR withdrew, the country became a veritable jungle. There was no law; the militias did anything that they wanted. Rwanda was a country without any law or official authority. People who knew that they were going to be killed and had some money went so far as to pay their killers to shoot them, preferring the bullet to being hacked or beaten to death. When UNAMIR was withdrawn, I heard that there were people at the United Nations who were saying that they couldn't send their soldiers to be killed at the end of the earth without a good reason. This leads me to wonder about what humanity is, about who is included in humanity and who is excluded. Why didn't the United Nations consider the people of Rwanda to be part of the humanity it is bound to protect? I haven't found an answer to this question yet.

LAZARE NAZARO, MEMBER OF THE MINISTRY OF REHABILITATION

I was in Kigali before and during the events of April 1994. I did not directly witness the killings here, but I saw many survivors who had been saved by the RPF. During this period, some of the members of the RPF who had come to Kigali to take part in the broad-based transitional government that had been negotiated in the Arusha accords were evacuated by RPF soldiers. Others stayed to help those who had survived the massacres. I decided to stay and assist wherever my help was needed.

Many survivors arrived in horrible condition. They were hardly human any more; they were barely recognizable. I saw horrific things and heard testimony about things that were even worse. I listened to a young boy who told me that he had been mutilated; the militia had cut him all over his body. He managed to escape and found a hiding place in some bushes near his home. From the bushes where he was hiding he saw militia members and soldiers rape his mother until she died. He was so frightened that he continued to hide. When he saw dogs come to eat his mother's body, he could not move to chase them away because he was afraid that the militia would see where he was hiding.

There are thousands of stories just like this one or worse. I did not come here to tell stories but to raise consciousness of the events that happened in Rwanda and raise the issue of the negligence of the international community during this period. Rwanda needed the international community at this time, and the international community was not there to help. Rwanda is a part of the international community, yet no one did anything to help.

We know the origins of this idea of exterminating the Tutsis, the idea of eliminating an entire group of people, but the political opposition was also exterminated. Newspapers and magazines published before the start of the genocide clearly show the extent of the extremism of the people in power. In certain meetings, such as the meeting of the *Mouvement Révolutionnaire National pour le Développement*[6] (MRND) in the subprefecture of Kabgaye on 22 November 1992, the extremists incited their followers to genocide by saying that the opponents of the MRND would exterminate members of the MRND if these opponents were not killed first. It was Léon Mugesera who said this to his followers. This was translated from Kinyarwanda into French and English and other languages, and everyone read about it in the newspaper *Kangura*.[7]

There were many other articles that appeared in the extremist press, but perhaps the most striking was the "Hutu Ten Commandments."[8] The international community saw all of this, they read the translations, and they listened to the hate broadcasts of RTLM. There were also documents that outlined the Habyarimana regime's extremist policy toward the Tutsis that came directly from the headquarters of the army chief of staff. For example, on page two of the "Hutu Ten Commandments," which was intended for high-ranking members of the chief of staff's office and for all the heads of sector, it says, "The principal enemy of the people of Rwanda is the Tutsi. From the inside or from the outside of the country, the Tutsi are extremists nostalgic for power. They have never recognized the reality of the social revolution of 1959 and they want to retake power by any means."

We were here to see everything being prepared. We saw it all start. And yet no one intervened. There were thousands and thousands of bodies in the streets, bodies floating down rivers, washing up on the shores of lakes, and all the while the international community was pursuing an academic debate over whether this constituted genocide or was simply a number of massacres. All of this discourse did nothing for the Rwandan people, and the killing continued. We said to ourselves, what is it that Rwanda has done to the rest of the world that they should abandon us like this?

I would like to emphasize that this genocide was not caused by ethnic hatred, as some people would like the world to believe. It was planned in advance to serve the interests of a small group of people. I can't say that these were political interests. If it had been a question of politics, there were a thousand other ways to reach the same goal. The genocide was planned and executed to serve the interests of a small clique of individuals.

■ EMMANUEL NGOMIRARONKA, DIRECTOR, HOPE UNLIMITED

I am currently the director of a nongovernmental organization, Hope Unlimited, that is focused on the defense of the rights of children, but I am a lawyer by training. Before the war, Hope Unlimited had in its care 49 infants and children, ranging in age from small babies to adolescents up to 15 years old, at a center in Kacyiru, a neighborhood in Kigali. I was responsible for the well-being of these children. When the fighting started on 6 April 1994, as the presidential guard, the army, and the militias were killing people all over Rwanda, I continued to receive orphans who were separated from their parents or whose parents had been killed. Between 6 and 11 April 1994, the RPF strengthened its positions around the capital. Around 11 April, the RPF forces arrived close to our center. Between 6 April and 26 May, I received an additional 71 children, which brought the total number of children in my care to 120. These children lived in miserable conditions, mostly because I did not have the facilities to look after more than 49, and especially because there was a war going on, food and clothing were scarce, and there was no other assistance available.

Daily the militias threatened the center, saying that I was caring for "RPF accomplices." Until 26 May there had been no direct attacks on the children. After 20 May, there were no longer any government troops between our center and the RPF lines, less than two kilometers from the center. However, there was still fighting going on, mainly with heavy weapons. On 26 May, at about 8:10 P.M., while the children were asleep, a militia that was too large for me to count attacked the six houses of our compound. Among the militia there were a number of soldiers in uniform. The militia were armed with guns, grenades, machetes, knives, and clubs. I was in a large house with my father, my two sisters, one of my brothers, and 25 of the children. The militia threw grenades into the other houses and soon afterward entered to kill the survivors. Suddenly, five militia members broke into the house where I was. They attacked my father and one of my brothers with their machetes, killing them on the spot. I ran out the back door with about 25 children following me.

It was around 9:00 P.M. and it was very dark. We ran down the hill toward the RPF lines two kilometers away. There was a swamp between our hill and the hill where the RPF was, so I had no other choice than to go through the swamp. I had never crossed the swamp and didn't know whether the water was too deep to cross or not. Despite everything, I told myself that even if I could save only five children, I had no other choice but to cross the swamp. We walked through the swamp with many of the children up to their waists in the water. We tried five different paths, each of which was too deep to manage. The younger and smaller children had a very hard time walking in the swamp, with their feet getting stuck in the mud and the water up to and above their chests. Finally, we found a path where the water was not as deep. We crossed it with great difficulty, the children struggling to keep their heads above the water and to move as quickly as they could. The whole time we were crossing the swamp, the government troops on the hill behind us were firing with heavy weapons over our heads at the RPF positions and the RPF was returning fire. As the shooting was going back and forth in both directions, we passed through the no-man's land in the middle.

We did not know exactly where we would find the RPF soldiers. We continued to walk through banana fields and swamps searching for the RPF. Along the way we saw many dead bodies in the banana fields. When we finally emerged from the fields, we found a small road. We followed the road, and in less than ten minutes we were stopped by two RPF soldiers. They ordered us to put our hands in the air, which we did. As they came closer, they asked me where we were coming from. I told them our story and explained that there might be more children at the center who had survived the attack and could not escape to follow us. The soldiers then told us to put our arms down and to follow them. They took us to a house a good distance away from the road where we emerged from the swamp. At that house they presented us to their lieutenant.

Towards 11 in the evening, the lieutenant told me that I was to accompany the RPF troops to the orphanage and told me that we would leave together at 4:00 A.M. At the appointed time we returned to the center with nine soldiers and their lieutenant without encountering any difficulties on the way. We found that the buildings had been completely destroyed and many of the children had been hacked to death with machetes. Searching through the bodies, we found 10 children who had hidden among the dead and had not been harmed. I also found one of my brothers who was seriously wounded by machete blows, but was still alive. The soldiers helped put my brother on a stretcher, and we carried him back to the RPF camp with the 10 surviving children. On the way back we noticed that many of the bodies of the children and caregivers had been burned, many of the houses looted, and there were burned documents strewn everywhere.

When we arrived back at the RPF hill in Gisozi, I had 35 children with me. On 29 May, we left Gisozi on foot and headed for Nyacyonga, escorted by soldiers from the RPF. The next day, we left Nyacyonga for Ndera, a smaller village about 17 kilometers from Kigali. In leaving Nyacyonga, the RPF allowed us to use a bus that had been taken from the government troops. On 31 May we were sent to another center where I continued to receive many children. Soon after, I had 552 children in my care.

I want to tell you about the suffering of these children. Some had watched the soldiers and militia murder their mothers and fathers or were mutilated themselves. Many of these children were wounded both physically and mentally. These children have suffered so much, yet they were innocent victims. These children have seen many atrocities. They are the living victims of the genocide. Children were abused and killed like anyone else, children received machete blows to their heads, children were shot, children were stoned, children were executed after listening to long speeches proclaimed in front of them about why they must be killed as accomplices—children were witness to all these heinous and bloody events.

In conclusion, I must say that this genocide, which did not spare the elderly, the innocent, or the children who had nothing to do with the politics of extremism, must be documented. Rwanda's genocide and its perpetrators and planners must be punished to the greatest extent of the law for the atrocities they committed against the innocent and against humankind.

▨ JEANNE KADALIKA UWONKUNDA, PROFEMME/TWESE HAMWE

At the beginning of the genocide, it was only men and male children who were killed, because they were seen as accomplices to the RPF and because in Rwandan society it is the man who has the right of land ownership. Women were not initially targeted but had to witness the torture and brutal killings of their husbands, sons, and brothers.

Soon after, they began attacking women, realizing that women gave life to the Tutsis' sons, fathers, and brothers. Women were subject to all sorts of torture; they were raped, burned alive, or buried alive. Women were also raped by large groups of soldiers and militia. The soldiers and militia did the most they could to humiliate the woman, raping her in front of her husband and children, then killing her children and her husband in front of her before taking her life.

Women and young girls were also taken away and locked up in homes by militias as their private property. The militia members referred to this action as "taking a wife." The militia member would then come back and rape the woman or girl whenever he wanted. Some women were threatened by their Hutu husband or by the husband's family because they were Tutsi or even because they resembled a Tutsi. With the advance of the RPF, husbands would sometimes abandon their Tutsi wives and family and flee for the border so they would not have problems at the roadblocks.

Women were powerless in the face of the genocide. Now, after the genocide, when you see women who have survived, you must realize that they have many problems. They are morose because they were powerless and could do nothing to stop the killing, but they also suffered all sorts of torture and trauma. Some were mutilated and cannot accept their own bodies. Some girls and women who were raped by the militias are now pregnant and will soon be having the children of their attackers. They are in despair and do not know what they will do with these children. Some might wish to abandon or kill the child; others may simply wish to kill themselves.

The genocide affected all Rwandans, but women in particular were deeply affected. Women had to witness the murder of their families. Many women have emotionally died because they were forced to watch as their families were killed. Many women were raped and they must now bear the pain of the horrors in the permanent form of a child. We must deal with the impact of the genocide, particularly the impact it has had on Rwandan women. We must find solutions to the problems resulting from the horror that has swept Rwanda.

Notes

1. Pledging conference held by international donor governments and the government of Rwanda to discuss funding for Rwandan government development initiatives.

2. United Nations Assistance Mission for Rwanda, deployed to Rwanda beginning 1 November 1993 as a part of the Arusha Peace Accords. UNAMIR and the UNAMIR mandate are further explained in Chapter 6.

3. Arusha Peace Accords, negotiated in Arusha, Tanzania, between the former government of Rwanda, the Rwandan Patriotic Front, and the other political parties in Rwanda. Signed in August 1993, the Arusha Accords put an end to the war between the former government and the RPF that began on 1 October 1990. The accords included a detailed plan for transition to multiparty democracy in Rwanda.

4. UN Security Council Resolution 955 (1994) established the International Criminal Tribunal for the Prosecution of Persons Responsible for Genocide and Other Serious Violations of International Humanitarian Law Committed in the Territory of Rwanda Between 1 January 1994 and 31 December 1994. The tribunal itself is based in The Hague. Trials will be held in Arusha, Tanzania. See Chapter 5 for a complete description.

5. *Radio-Télévision Libre des Mille Collines* (Thousand Hills Free Radio-Television) was a privately owned and operated extremist broadcasting system established by members of the former government of Rwanda and President Habyarimana's wife as the active "voice" of extremism. RTLM was endorsed by and received indirect support from the former government of Rwanda.

6. National Revolutionary Movement for Development was the political party of President Habyarimana and the sole state party until multiparty democracy was allowed by the Constitution of 1991.

7. Independent extremist journal published in Kigali.

8. Originally published in *Kangura*; see Chapter 4 for a complete translation.

CHAPTER

HISTORICAL AND POLITICAL PERSPECTIVES ON THE GENOCIDE

Introduction

■ ALAIN SIGG, PUBLIC AFFAIRS OFFICER, UNITED NATIONS INTERNATIONAL CRIMINAL TRIBUNAL FOR RWANDA

> *In the corrupted currents of this world*
> *Offence's gilded hand may shove by justice,*
> *And oft 'tis seen the wicked prize itself*
> *Buys out the law. But it is not so above;*
> *There is no shuffling, there the action lies*
> *In his true nature, and we ourselves compelled,*
> *Even to the teeth and forehead of our faults*
> *To give in evidence.*
>
> Hamlet, III, iii

Searching for the truth is a long-term process when compared with the swiftness with which we commit a guilty deed. Memory—collective memory—is the foundation of this process. Just months after the beginning of the Rwandan tragedy, we are already concerned that this memory is fading: Some witnesses to the horror have already left or are about to leave Rwanda; some are tired of remembering; others have cut themselves off from the past in order to cope with the present. Time might be a healer, but forgetfulness is not.

Naming this conference "Genocide: A Collective Memory" meant inviting the unpredictable. In remembering an event such as the genocide in Rwanda, reason and emotion are necessarily commingled, and indeed they were at the conference. Like the rest of this book, the following chapter on historical and political perspectives is a mosaic of thoughts, with each section being a combination of the speaker's memory and spontaneous reaction to the previous speaker. This mosaic will enable the reader to understand what Shakespeare called "the true nature" of the "action" through different testimonies, thereby avoiding any "shuffling." This is the classic platonic approach to truth and knowledge, and is certainly the clearest path to truth and knowledge in a society that, like Rwanda's, is based on oral tradition.

Before moving into the history of Rwanda, some major issues should be emphasized. When pictures of the horror in Rwanda appeared on our television screens, there was a tendency to forget the universal nature of the barbarity, to rationalize it away as though Rwanda were a forlorn African country and the genocide was another example of base primitivism and ethnic hatred worthy only of our pity. This, of course, is completely wrong. It takes time to understand how refined and deeply cultured Rwandan society was and still is; it takes time to understand how cultural sophistication can coexist with such barbarity; and it takes time to imagine that a genocidal ideology can only be developed by intellectuals—certainly not by impoverished peasants.[1]

Time is the Achilles' heel for both expatriates and journalists of all countries arriving in postgenocide Rwanda. When the moon rises, we realize that we have spent our day sending a fax or finding a crucial spare part—and after a few new moons, at best, we leave the country. We leave behind the silent stars of Rwanda under which, less than one century ago, the wise *Abiru*[2] knew the rules and customs by heart, acting as a supreme court to control and balance the power of the king. In 1930, when the first Western historians asked the *Abiru* to relate his knowledge of Rwanda, his narrative lasted for months. We also leave behind our Rwandan friends who can personally trace their family histories back for five generations and who know this family tree by heart as it was passed on in the oral tradition. And with them we leave questions: How will the next generation fill the narrative void caused by genocide? How will they be able to learn about their origins when their whole family has been murdered?

Historians have been attempting for half a century to explain the coexistence of culture and barbarity, the roots of fascism and its appalling consequences. Yet they have been unable to provide us with an ultimate answer to the question of how people could simultaneously listen to Beethoven played by the urbane Berlin Philharmonic and to the bombs falling on Berlin—all the while aware of atrocities being perpetrated on German soil. I will leave it to others to explore whether genocide can occur only among "refined" societies.

Basically—and paradoxically—Rwanda is a homogeneous society: Rwandans share the same cultural tradition, the same music, the same dances, and the same religion (92 percent are Christians). Most of all, Kinyarwanda is a language common to all Rwandans; there are linguistic variations according to certain regions, but no major differences among dialects. In Rwanda, there has never been an upper class *lingua franca* or any other linguistic differentiation. We often tend to forget that a common language also means common wit and repartee, common allegories, and, most of all, common wisdom and proverbs. I would like to quote a proverb that is particularly significant in respect to what happened in 1994: *"Useka umuturanyi ukabyuka musa"* ("You laugh at your neighbor, but in the morning you get up as he does"). As we know, the Twa, the Hutus, and the Tutsis used to, and still do, live together on the same hills. The word "neighbor" in this proverb therefore represents a nondivisive concept of ethnicity; and yet "neighbors" killed each other during the tragic months of 1994.

If we add up all of the inhabitants and refugees from Rwanda and Burundi, we could state that about 15 million people speak the same language—an exceptional situation in Africa. In many respects, Rwanda, and even the whole African Great Lakes region, is more unified and homogenous than, for example, Switzerland. We should always bear in mind this reality when we think of solutions in Rwanda; the common language should be a key factor in any political approach to a regional, global solution for peace in the Great Lakes region.

Language played a distinct role in the Rwandan crisis. It is essential to be particularly cautious and reflect carefully on the meaning of concepts and their semantic connotations. Gérard Prunier is justified in thinking that the Hutus and the Tutsis were probably two distinct ethnic groups that time has culturally homogenized (but *not* unified) and biologically mingled (but *not* amalgamated).[3] Confusing these concepts easily carries us into the world of semantic manipulation or into Orwell's "doublethink" from the novel *1984*. This kind of manipulation was used by President Habyarimana in his speech on 5 July 1973, at the dawn of the Second Republic, after his coup d'état and the massacres of the Tutsi population: "I have come to bring you peace, unity and reconciliation." The result was that, once more, thousands among the Tutsi population fled into Uganda.

We ought to be careful with the word "reconciliation," as it has been used and misused too frequently. According to Rwandan tradition, *kwiyunga* (reconciliation) is a privilege that the victim is free to bestow, but only after the offender has asked for *gusaba imbabzi* (pardon). In recent history, this has rarely happened in Rwanda—on the contrary, the offender was rather praised, escaping unpunished in a culture of impunity.

The ideological preparation of genocide reveals an even more sordid manipulation of language and doublethink. As in any totalitarian tradition, imagery and metaphors to encourage horror were borrowed both from the noble parts of the country's history and from the agrarian world. *Interahamwe*, a distinguished group of men known for their solidarity in Rwandan history, became the name for a ruthless gang of thugs killing with machetes. *Inyenzi*, meaning cockroaches, was the name given to the soldiers of the RPF—and, of course, cockroaches were to be eliminated, like the "stinking seed" during the Cultural Revolution in China.

The agrarian metaphors used to mobilize the population were often cruel. For example, *gukorra* means "to work" in Kinyarwanda; during the genocide it meant "to kill"—a poignant reminder of expressions such as *Arbeit macht frei* ("Work makes freedom") that were used in Nazi concentration camps. In both cases, the individual killer's conscience was disassociated from his acts: Killing simply became "working," an 8-to-5 job with a break for lunch.[4] As in other totalitarian regimes, language was a barrier rather than a bridge between conscience and deed. Pity itself, universally connected to grief and affliction, became a synonym for killing in the "Hutu Ten Commandments"—a nefarious plagiarism of the Holy Book. The eighth commandment reads, "The Hutu must no longer have pity on the Tutsi."[5]

In Rwanda, where words such as "pity" and the "Ten Commandments" have been so corrupted, the word "guilt" also needs to be redefined. Acknowledging guilt before asking for pardon is the postulate to any reconciliation. Men and women of faith, both inside and outside of the Church, have a huge educational role in this process. Without them, the reign of doublethink cannot come to an end.

In this process, the didactic impact of national and particularly of international justice should not be neglected. In a country with a tradition of impunity, punishing the guilty will contribute to a redefinition of guilt and help to reestablish the moral standards that years of totalitarian manipulation have eradicated. Those involved in future trials as magistrates and witnesses will, moreover, keep a collective memory alive and prevent the horrors of the genocide from sinking into forgetfulness. Through the process of justice, both the mourning survivors and the judicial system will listen to testimonies that lead to the truth. History will be rewritten not only in books, but also in our minds. Through the trials, those grieving will at least be able to know some of the missing links in the chain of their personal history and, through this knowledge, to soothe some of their pain. Justice will at least be able to convey the message that a crime against humanity is a universal crime, that certain moral standards of the old *jus cogens* (rule of law) govern the world—and not sordid vested interests.

Rwandans and their friends are desperately awaiting this symbolic moment, although we all know that it can only be the beginning of healing: "*Inkoni ivuna igufwa, ntivuna ingeso*" ("The stick breaks bones, not vices," or "punishment alone does not lead to conversion"). Justice has always conveyed hope, particularly the hope of a fairer, more righteous world. Rwanda desperately needs hope to balance the loss caused by the horror of genocide—and as we know, hope can move mountains.

Quantifying the role that the Nuremberg trials played in reestablishing peace and stability in Europe is impossible. Yet to assert that it did not have a role is also impossible. For the postwar generation, "never again" is endowed with a very precise meaning; indeed, we have never experienced the inconceivable inhumanity that our fathers experienced. The ideal of "never again," of tolerance, has gone through climax and anticlimax, but has remained strong enough to prevent or at least to hinder the worst forms of overt discrimination.

We shall not leave the subject of justice without considering one of its master critics, Franz Kafka. In *The Trial*, Joseph K. is told one morning by two foreigners in uniform that he is guilty, although he never learns why. During the genocide, Rwandans had to show identity cards listing their ethnic group (a colonial act of ingenuity) at roadblocks across the country. The verdict was prompt: If you were Tutsi you were immediately selected to be killed, raped, or both. Kafka's existentialism and his notion of the absurd became very tangible in April 1994 Rwanda: Your culpability? Your crime? To be born a Tutsi. Or simply to be born.

When questioning survivors who were taken to specific places such as churches[6] to be killed as to why they had not reacted, rebelled, or resisted, the author of the present text was answered, "*Parce que nous étions morts avants.*" ("Because we were already dead beforehand.") How can we understand this? Again, Joseph K. comes to mind: At the end of *The Trial*, he finally sees his executioners in front of him. There is no reaction, no stirring, but rather relief. He, too, has died beforehand.

Colonialism and the Churches as Agents of Ethnic Division

■ **DR. JEAN DAMASCENE NDAYAMBAJE WITH JEAN MUTABARUKA, PROFESSORS, NATIONAL UNIVERSITY OF RWANDA**

The Colonialists

The first European to set foot in Rwanda, a German, arrived in May 1894. Before then, Rwanda had been described as a land of mystery, home of the source of the Nile and the Mountains of the Moon. When the first Europeans arrived in Rwanda they found a politically and socially well-organized kingdom. Europeans had never seen such a well-organized kingdom in Africa, so they assumed that the people of

Rwanda must have come from another continent—that they were, in fact, Hamites from Egypt. In no small way, this was the first step toward genocide.

At the Conference of Berlin[7] in 1884 and 1885, Germany was given a protectorate that included Rwanda, Burundi, and Tanzania. After realizing that the kingdom of Rwanda was well organized and heavily populated, the German colonial administration instituted a system of indirect rule. While the machinery of royal power was maintained, a representative from the German colonial administration was placed at the side of the king of Rwanda. Gradually, the Rwandan *mwami*[8] was transformed into a simple bureaucrat. However, Germany's plans for Rwanda did not come to fruition, as German rule lasted only until 1916.

At the end of the First World War, Germany's colonies in Africa were split up among the Allied Powers, and Belgium was given control of Rwanda. The prewar administrative structure of the Germans was modified by the Belgian colonial authorities in 1926. Major Declerk, following the guidelines of his mission, implemented a policy of indirect administration. The Belgian minister of colonies described this policy as follows: "It is decided that in Rwanda and Burundi, where there exists a well-structured and powerful indigenous authority, the relationship of the metropole with these territories should be that of indirect administration. Power over the indigenous population will rest, in principle, in the hands of the indigenous supreme chief of each of these provinces to whom will be assigned, as a counselor and eventually a tutor, a European representative named by the government of the metropole."

The minister of colonies believed that the role of the colonial administration should be limited to controlling, guiding, and developing the function of traditional institutions. In practice, this policy was carried out through the massive recruitment of Tutsis and their posting to different territorial services. This reliance on the Tutsis, in part a consequence of the policy of indirect rule, was also based on an erroneous conviction, propagated by the writings of missionaries, that stated that the Tutsis were better suited to rule than the Hutus. To their own detriment, this was a conviction that the Tutsis themselves ended up believing.

The Belgian colonial administration consolidated three precolonial *cheferie* (chieftancies)—those of army, cattle, and agriculture—under a

single Tutsi chief. Before colonialism, and under the German protectorate, these chieftancies were not divided along ethnic lines. The chief
of cattle was historically always a Tutsi, but the chief of the army or the
chief of agriculture could be either a Hutu or a Tutsi. In uniting these
three chieftancies under a single Tutsi chief, the Belgians created an
administrative system based on ethnic discrimination.

The Belgian system of ethnic segregation was permanently
installed in 1931 with the removal by Belgian colonial authorities
of King Musinga. His replacement, the Belgian-approved King
Rudahigwa, was forced to adapt to the colonial system. Tutsis were
soon after named to head all chieftancies, effectively spreading the
political power of the Tutsi chiefs across the entire country. The new
local chiefs were obliged to collaborate with the colonialists, who began
to require more and more forced labor from the population. As intermediaries for the colonial power, the Tutsi chiefs became the primary
target for the resentments of the local population.

It is worth underlining that it was the Germans who, as the first to
arrive in Rwanda, created the first system of ethnic classification among
Rwandan tribal groups, based on 19th-century racial typologies. The
colonialists could not believe that the Tutsis and Hutus were of the
same tribe, or even that the Tutsis were Africans. They searched for
"scientific" explanations by measuring the height, nose, and forehead
size of the Tutsis. German anthropologists eventually discovered that
there was no morphological difference between Hutus and Tutsis and
that their supposition that the two were different races was false.

The Belgians imitated the Germans in accentuating the differences
between the ethnic groups that composed Rwandan society. Despite
scientific proof that Hutus and Tutsis are of the same genetic stock, the
Belgians insisted well into the 1950s that the Tutsis were Hamites,
descendants of Ham and members of an ancient race that blended
white and black. This false racial classification put the Tutsis in the position of being foreign invaders in their own country and exposed them
to an eventual ethnic and nationalist backlash from Hutus who were
pejoratively classified as the aboriginal population of Rwanda.

The Belgian colonial policy of exclusive support for one ethnic
group was an infringement on the rights and liberties of both individuals and the community. Worse still, the Belgian colonial administration instituted, in 1933, a system of identity cards that listed the

bearer's ethnic group: Hutu, Tutsi, or Twa. As they had little other basis upon which to make a distinction, the Belgians used the arbitrary economic criteria of cattle ownership to determine an individual's ethnic group. A person who owned more than 10 cattle was classified as Tutsi, one who owned fewer was classified as Hutu. The Twa were classified according to their occupation as potters and hunters and received little other consideration. On this basis, the Belgians issued identity cards to all Rwandans. From this moment forward tribal identity became hereditary, passing from a father to his children, and creating an irreparable cleavage in Rwandan society.

From 1945 to 1962, the United Nations placed Rwanda under the trusteeship of the Belgians, who were given responsibility for moving the country toward self-administration and independence. In 1952, the Belgian administration instituted a system of popular representation that called for the election of representative councils at each level of the political hierarchy. The first election of notable councils took place in 1953. The Belgian administrator, instead of considering the actual results of the election, took into account the number of people elected by ethnic group. The Belgian doctrine of ethnic separation interpreted the results of the elections in terms of possible future ethnic inequalities, thus making them a reality.

Rwandan politics were not immune to the growing movement of nationalist consciousness in Africa in the 1950s and 1960s. Belgian policy during this period made it very clear to the Hutus that to achieve independence they would have to first rid themselves of their "colonial invaders," the Tutsis. On the eve of independence, the Belgian government made the Tutsis the scapegoats for all the sufferings of Rwandans during the colonial period.

The Belgians broadcast their revisionist history and their racist policies through propaganda campaigns and through the mass media, converting many to their beliefs. The Hutu masses, encouraged by the Belgians, missionaries, and their own leaders, became conscious of their supposed inferior social status. In the height of the absurdity, they treated the Tutsis, not the Belgians, as "feudal colonialists," and they fought, not for independence from the Belgians, but for emancipation from the Tutsi "foreigners from Ethiopia."

The Belgian colonial administration manipulated the revolt of the Hutus, which was later called a revolution, but which quickly transformed into a series of massacres. At first the Tutsi elite were targeted, but later, Tutsi peasants also fell victim to the violence. It was in this climate of ethnic violence that Rwanda achieved independence.

The Missionaries

Missionaries first arrived in Rwanda in 1900 and worked hand in hand with the colonialists. The missionaries were divided into two camps in their approach to evangelization. To convert as many Rwandans as possible as quickly as possible, one group of missionaries chose to work with the Hutu peasants, whom they considered simple-minded and easily led to Christianity. The other group chose to work with the Tutsis, believing that if they converted the proud and independent Tutsis, they would easily be able to convert the rest of the country. The second group won.

An approach shared by all missionaries, Catholic and Protestant, was the evangelization of Rwanda through the teaching of "God's word." They created schools with the goal of converting both present and future generations of the population to Christianity. Writing in 1910, a Catholic missionary named R. P. Loupias was clear about his goals: "We will not have any scholars, but will be largely satisfied if, through schooling, we are able to train an enlightened Christian elite who will pass on the faith to those around them. The importance of schooling is not reading and writing, but religious instruction."[9]

Protestant missionaries arrived shortly after the Catholics, but shared the same objective in their schools. A Protestant missionary, G. Warneck, described the church's need for educated followers: "In order for the Protestant Church to function, it needs an indigenous clergy that all of the population respects and lay ministers capable of taking charge of the administration of the church. It will be impossible to reach this goal as long as the entire population has not achieved a minimum level of education, that will not happen without the aid of elementary schools. It is therefore unthinkable today to convert a people to Christianity without schooling."[10]

In evangelizing the Tutsis, the missionaries sought to create a Christian kingdom in the heart of Africa. When King Musinga refused to be baptized in 1931, he was dethroned by the Belgians and replaced with a king more amenable to the wishes of the Catholic Church. By the 1940s the Church had its Christian king, blessed by the Pope, and a symbiosis had been created among the Catholic Church, the colonial administration, and the government of Belgium. Ethnic divisions were ingrained in the colonial school system. A primary school was established solely for the sons of chiefs, which created tangible antagonism.

Later, for different historical reasons, the Catholics gained a monopoly over education in Rwanda at all levels (primary, secondary, and university).

The Churches: Disregard of Rights and Freedom in Rwanda

To achieve their mission of training a Christian elite, missionaries organized groups of indigenous lay people to work for the Catholic Church and for the newly formed colonial administration. As part of this approach they created seminaries and secondary schools. To gain as many converts as possible, it was also necessary to reach out to the ruling class, notably the court at the Royal City of Nyanza.

The founder of the White Fathers, Cardinal Lavigerie, left instructions to the members of his order first and foremost to win over the chiefs, who, once converted, would bring the rest of their tribe with them. But in Rwanda, several chiefs were hostile to the Church's evangelism. The missionaries, worried about the future of their new church in Rwanda, created a primary school for the sons of chiefs at Nyanza. They foresaw that sooner or later prejudice against the Church would diminish and that eventually bonds of friendship would develop between teachers and students. This school had the added advantage of facilitating the entry of missionaries into the political and aristocratic circles and allowed them to discretely evangelize the nobility of Rwanda.

After the end of the First World War, the Belgians defined the following objectives for the school at Nyanza: to instruct and educate the sons of chiefs in order to prepare them for their duties and to make them into enlightened auxiliaries of the church, to train administrators for government schools, and to train Tutsis to become priests.

Nonetheless, the Royal School at Nyanza was criticized by the missionaries themselves because the heterogeneous mix of married men, teenagers, and young boys created an amalgam of students who could not be supervised outside of the classroom. In addition, the school was located in what the missionaries considered bad surroundings, the Royal Court at Nyanza. Moved by a nationalist spirit, King Musinga was becoming more and more hostile to Christianity and to the influence of Europeans—and was recalcitrant in the face of the demands of the colonial administration. His resistance to the colonial administration and the Church eventually led to his being deposed by the Belgians in 1931. He was replaced by his son, King Rudahigwa, who had grown up under the influence of the Apostolic Vicar, Father Classé. The new king was converted to Christianity and baptized, which greatly facilitated the expansion of Catholicism in Rwanda.

The Royal School at Nyanza and four other schools, also strictly reserved for the sons of chiefs, served as catalysts for the evangelization of Rwanda. Fear of Protestant proselytizing led the Catholic Church to incorporate these schools into the educational system as independent subsidized schools. The Royal School at Nyanza was eventually suspended, transferred to Butare, and handed over to the leadership of the Belgian Brothers of the Charity of Gand. There was a firm resolve on the part of Catholic authorities to destroy all centers of secularism and to take charge of the training of the future elite of the country, who would preferably come from the ranks of the Tutsi aristocracy. The leaders of the Catholic Church believed that it was among the aristocracy in particular, and among the Tutsis in general, that they would find the most intelligent, fervent, and zealous students. The Church believed it had to trust the Tutsis because whoever won over the Tutsis would win over all of the people of Rwanda.

The missionaries limited the right to education to those they felt would serve the intellectual and cultural expansion of the Church. The creation of the missionary school system was one of the sources of ethnic division in Rwanda. The discriminatory policies of these schools were clear. As a result of these policies, the social origins of the so-called "civilized" students and their participation in European culture forced a greater and greater separation between the educated elite and the peasant masses. This situation created unmerited pride on the part of the students and a deep sense of resentment in the peasants.

As the independence movement spread across Africa, the United Nations criticized Belgium for its paternalistic colonial policy that kept the people of its colonies dependent upon Belgian largesse. In effect, Belgium had trained only a handful of local officials for higher office. The Catholic Church was also criticized for its monopoly over education.

Through a complex series of Machiavellian manipulations, certain missionary fathers were able to link the call for independence by Tutsi and Hutu nationalists with communism. According to these priests, the danger was clear and their need for support was pressing. At the same time, a virulent group of young Flemish separatist priests transplanted the Flemish separatist movement in Belgium to the Church in Rwanda. Feeling close to the oppressed peasants of Rwanda, the Flemish separatists decided to join their struggles. In fact, their political activism in support of the oppressed made them collaborators of the new oppressors.

The segregationist movement in the Rwandan Church was soon supported by a new Swiss bishop, Monsignor Perraudin, as a political subterfuge to incite the Hutus against their Tutsi compatriots. Perraudin was to become the pillar of the struggle between the ethnic groups in Rwanda. In fact, Perraudin portrayed Gregoire Kayibanda[11] as the strongest ally of Belgian colonialism. A cynical alliance developed between the colonial administration and the Catholic and Protestant missionaries to support the overthrow of the Tutsis. The roots of the genocide of the Tutsis date from this period.

In an interview in the newspaper *Le Journal de Genève* (17 April 1994), Monsignor Perraudin was asked about his silence regarding the genocide that was then taking place in Rwanda. His response was that he "condemns but understands." He condemns the genocide as a humanitarian and a Christian. He understands, as one who played a major role in the institutionalization of ethnic division in Rwanda, that his followers went too far, but feels that this could be justified following his segregationist doctrine. This is the same Perraudin who, in 1956, incited the Hutu to overthrow and chase into exile the Tutsis whose rise to power had been supported by his predecessors, Monsignors Hirth, Classé, and Deprimoz, at the beginning of the century.

Here the question arises: Who was responsible for the formation of the small group of extremist Hutu Catholics in the Gitarama prefecture who mobilized the masses to violence in the late 1950s? The Research Center on Socio-Political Information in Brussels (CRISP) stated in its African newsletter dated 5 February 1960 that "it is from the Catholic Center at Kabgaye (residence of Monsignor Perraudin) in the prefecture of Gitarama that Hutu propaganda has spread."

If I have insisted to such a degree on the total deficiency of the churches and the colonial authorities at the beginning of the bloody

events of 1959 in Rwanda, it is because at that time it was still possible
to avoid escalation of the conflict. This would have saved the lives of
thousands of innocent victims as well as the reputation of the Catholic
and Protestant churches in Rwanda and of the Belgians, who were later
forced to accept the deteriorating situation and the genocide in Rwanda
as a *fait accompli.*

In reality, it was between 1955 and 1958 that the Belgian colonial
administration in Rwanda, as well as the churches, completely reversed
their traditional policies and began to systematically support, by their
actions and inactions, the rise to power of a group of extremist
pseudointellectual Hutu politicians. The price of this support has been
the blood of thousands of innocent Tutsi men, women, and children.
The Tutsi king and chiefs of the time were seriously mistaken in their
estimate of the reaction of the Belgian authorities in Rwanda as well as
that of the Catholic and Protestant churches.

When the Hutus realized that the Tutsis had lost not only the support of the local Belgian authorities, but also that of the Catholic
Church, open hostility quickly replaced the traditional understanding
between the Tutsi sovereign, or *mwami*, and the Hutu masses. The
Hutu leadership judged that the moment was right to rid themselves
first of the traditional Tutsi powers, then of the Belgian colonialists.
The report of the International Commission of Inquiry on the unrest
in Rwanda of November 1959, dated 26 February 1960, stipulates
that "The Belgian authorities exercised a decisive impact on the
evolution of the unrest. . . . In certain chiefdoms in the north of
Rwanda, practically no Tutsi household was saved. The repression
organized by the Tutsi leadership was quickly suppressed by military
action undertaken by the Belgian government." This unequivocal
statement clearly shows the role of the colonial administration in the
Rwandan tragedy.

The Institutionalization of Ethnic Segregation

As a matter of policy, the first Europeans to arrive in Rwanda assigned
the Tutsis a genetic superiority over all the other tribal groups in
Rwanda. Together, the colonialists and the missionaries exploited the
Hamitic myth and the myth of Tutsi superiority to colonize and evangelize the Rwandan people. Constrained by their relations with the
colonialists, the traditional Tutsi chiefs were forced to constantly

increase taxes and require more forced labor from the population. It was these same chiefs who later became the first targets of the growing rancor of the peasant masses.

These policies revealed the egocentric and cynical acrobatics of moral self-protection that the colonialists and the Church used to rehabilitate the Hutus, whom for years they had oppressed through the Tutsis. It was during this bloody conflict between Hutus and Tutsis that the First Republic was born in 1962.

The First Republic and Its Quota System

On the eve of the foundation of the First Republic in Rwanda, the colonialists and the missionaries had already achieved their objective: to turn one group of Rwandans against another and thereby camouflage their own responsibility. This strategy permitted them to continue their activities in Rwanda in peace. They also succeeded in focusing the political debate on social revolution and ethnic emancipation rather than on nationalism and anticolonialism.

The case of Rwanda was largely an enigma for outside observers, including the United Nations. Why, at the time that all other African countries were calling for independence, did some Rwandans prefer to collaborate with the colonial power? The demagogy of the colonial school system and the obsession of the missionaries with the supposed communist threat took their toll on the Tutsis on the eve of independence.

In response to every query by the international community about what was happening in Rwanda, the Belgian colonialists provided figures on ethnic inequalities in the administration, and the missionaries presented statistics demonstrating the social inequalities in their schools. Yet it was these supposed defenders of human rights who caused these inequalities. The international community simply did not understand. The lack of truthfulness of the Belgian colonial administration and the bad faith of the churches were later revealed, but by that time it was too late.

A petition by Rwandan students in Lovanium (presently Kinshasa) is a case in point:

> Concerning the cultural monopoly of the Tutsi, that is an
> immediate effect of the educational system, how can one explain

the large percentage of Tutsi students, and how can one present it as the fault of the Tutsis, when the management of the school system is in the hands of the missionaries and the colonial administration? And above all, how is it that it is only after forty years that this anomaly has been noticed? Doubtless the time is right for the colonial administration to confess the sins of the Tutsi in order to avoid the imminent attack of two million Hutus, left until now in complete and abject destitution.[12]

These inequalities were the consequence of Belgian colonial policy in Rwanda, and the colonial administration had to act quickly to destroy any compromising evidence. Therefore it created chaos in the name of social revolution, and advised the newly created regime to install a system of quotas in the school system and in employment in order to remedy the same racist policies it had been implementing for years.

The Bahutu Manifesto,[13] also known as the Hutu Manifesto or the PARMEHUTU Manifesto, was published on 24 March 1957, declaring the need for a system of ethnic quotas to compensate for the injustice done to the Hutus in the past. The text of the manifesto, referring to the use of identity cards to respect ethnic quotas, outlined the segregationist policies that were followed by the subsequent governments of Rwanda. It should have served as a warning for those who sought to understand the educational and administrative policies of newly independent Rwanda.

As a justification of their policy of issuing ethnic identity cards, the future leaders of Rwanda cited the risk of continued bias favoring the Tutsis over the Hutus and the need to base ethnic statistics on accurate numbers. In actuality, their intent in revealing ethnicity on identification cards was to identify the Tutsis anywhere—at school, in the office, in a taxi, or even on the street. This identification would also facilitate the elimination of the Tutsis when the moment came. On the eve of the genocide in Rwanda, one finds the same arguments against the elimination of the use of ethnicity on identity cards. The supporters of this system counted on, and did in fact use, this as a tool for identifying Tutsis to be slaughtered.

The founders of the PARMEHUTU[14] party called for maintaining the ethnicity of the bearer on identity cards for unavowed but deeply held reasons, justified in the following terms by Fidele Nkundabagenzi:

The children of those people who, between 1920 and 1959, were
forced to perform unpaid community labor were allowed to
pursue their studies through the end of high school free of
charge. Every school identity card was marked Hutu, Tutsi or
Twa in order to inform those who were combating racial
discrimination in the schools.[15]

In the mass of people forced to perform community labor, one
wonders whether the PARMEHUTU included the poor Tutsi peasants
who did not have the benefits of the privileges the colonialists gave to
the Tutsi aristocracy. One must also wonder whether anyone can truly
combat racial and ethnic discrimination through another person.

The PARMEHUTU party did not specify for how long these measures would be in place. Later, PARMEHUTU based its power on ethnic
segregation and the exclusion of Tutsis at every level of government
administration. Moreover, with each incursion by Tutsi exiles, hatred of
the Tutsis cemented itself in the consciousness of the Hutus, provoking
innumerable massacres. In December 1963 alone, less than a year and
a half after independence, more than 10,000 Tutsis were slaughtered.

Racism was so prevalent at the time that human rights violations
took place even in public. The following is an eloquent example: "In
the time of Kayibanda, it was common to see posters on the walls of
schools, hospitals and public enterprises that said tersely: 'The Tutsis
whose names follow are requested, from today onwards, to no longer
set foot in this office.'"[16] The same author emphasized the following:
"Independent Rwanda defined its identity in denying the right to existence of the other, in defining as a foreigner those [the Tutsi] who were
their [the Hutus'] interior double."[17]

The anxiety that fed hatred of the Tutsis was prevalent everywhere.
In the cultural domain, traditional cultural celebrations were banned to
avoid the artistic influence of the Tutsis. Figurative art, which is most
typically Tutsi, was to have no place in independent Rwanda. The people of Rwanda would have to be satisfied with baroque missionary art,
embroidery, weaving, *papier coupé*—in sum, childish art forms without
symbolic significance. Freedom of expression in art and speech were no
longer permitted.

In the school system, the Education Bill of 1966 was directed
(without clearly stating the goal) against the Catholic Church and Tutsi

domination of the priesthood and of teaching. Since independence on 1 July 1962 the Tutsis were systematically denied scholarships to the National University of Rwanda and for study abroad, with only a few exceptions. Tutsis were excluded from the army. The segregationist policy of the army went to great lengths to discriminate against Hutus married to Tutsis. The irony of this policy of Hutu ethnic purification is that the Kayibanda regime ended up supporting its own gravediggers. Many individuals who were influential in the persecution of Tutsis in the First Republic also took part in the overthrow of the Kayibanda regime.

Despite all the unpleasantness of newly independent Rwanda, the international community did nothing to denounce the Kayibanda regime's drift toward ethnic exclusion. The human rights abuses suffered by the Tutsis at the time were committed in the name of populism and the rule of the majority, a policy that hardly masked the racism that inspired it. The hypocrisy of the situation was hard to conceal and took place with the complicity of the churches and of the international community. During the First Republic, the angry outbursts of the party were always accompanied by pogroms against the Tutsis.

The writer Alexis Curver wrote in *The Martyrdom of the Tutsis*,

> It is no longer the small progressive bulletins in my diocese that publish . . . bitter homage to the kind Hutus. It is everyone. It seems as if the evil Tutsis, displaced, despoiled and crowded into camps, are a menace to public order. It is probably true, but this is the same thing that Hitler said of the Jews.[18]

Toward 1972, the First Republic could no longer deal with the basic problems of the country because of the paralysis caused by its segregationist policies and by interregional tensions within the PARMEHUTU party. Profiting from ethnic tensions in neighboring Burundi, President Kayibanda made the Tutsis a scapegoat under the pretext that they were trying to take power and eliminate him. The Tutsis were accused of causing all of the problems that PARMEHUTU and the government could not resolve.

In the schools and in the university, Hutu students were turned against their Tutsi classmates and teachers. The elimination of the Tutsis was said to be the solution to the growing problem of unemployment. The cyclical nature of these massacres can be seen in the curious fact that a large number of the students who organized and executed the massacre of Tutsis in the secondary schools and universities in 1972 and 1973 were later found among the leadership of the Second Republic. These same former students were also the instigators of the genocide in 1994. It is sufficient to mention the following: Léon Mugesera, former professor at the National University of Rwanda and member of President Habyarimana's MRND party;[19] Ferdinand Nahimana, founder of Radio RTLM; Pastor Musabe, brother of the infamous Theoneste Bagosora, former colonel in the Rwandan army; Jerome Bicamumpaka, foreign minister of the genocidal regime; Stanislas Mbonampeka, minister of justice of the same government; and one of the many leaders of the genocide, Jean Kambanda.

From the university, to the high schools, to the public institutions of Rwanda, anti-Tutsi sentiments moved quickly to the private sector, where many employers and business owners were obliged to fire their Tutsi employees. In the seminaries, a number of Tutsi priests and nuns were killed and others were permanently exiled to neighboring countries. In February 1973, attacks on Tutsi peasants began in earnest. Tutsis were chased down and killed, their houses burned, and their belongings stolen. Juvenal Habyarimana, then chief of the army and minister of national defense, put an end to this disorder by staging a coup that overthrew President Kayibanda and led the military to power.

The Second Republic: Ethnic and Regional Equilibrium

After the military coup d'état of 5 July 1973, General Juvenal Habyarimana proclaimed himself president of the Second Republic.[20] He undertook to put an end to what he considered a policy of demagoguery and dissension. He declared that he had come to save a country that was about to be pushed into a bottomless chasm by a band of tired and irresponsible politicians. But once again, the new president, the "savior" of Rwanda, ensured that the perpetrators of the massacres went unpunished. These are the same people who were to become members of the president's own party and who later organized the genocide of 1994.

After founding the Second Republic in the name of peace and national unity, Habyarimana spoke of national reconciliation and seemed to want an end to the persecution of the Tutsis. The Tutsis greeted him as a savior. He preached the ideology of development, undertook a good-neighbor policy with the bordering states, and called for all the sons and daughters of Rwanda to "bring their own small stone" to help in the construction of the nation.

The marriage of Habyarimana to Agathe Kanziga, descendant of one of the most powerful Hutu chiefs of the north of the country, was a determining factor in his failure as a president. His wife's powerful family "brought him back to reason," reminding him of his ethnic and regional roots. This eventually led to the establishment of the *Akazu*[21] and of Network Zero.[22]

To better govern the nation, Habyarimana announced his policy of ethnic and regional equilibrium. What was not clear at the time, but later became amply apparent, was that Habyarimana wanted to create an autocratic regime by segregating the Tutsis and those he called the "southern demagogues," who were none other than members of the government that he had just overthrown.

In the face of this policy of exclusion, the Tutsis and other marginalized groups from the south tried to surmount the obstacles placed in their path by first creating private schools and later creating private scholarships for their children to attend the National University. Tutsis would never be eligible to receive scholarships to study abroad. In their exclusion, the Tutsis dedicated themselves to activities, such as commerce, that were not under government control.

Rwanda's dictator issued double-speak pronouncements to his followers, saying that everything was for the best in the best of all possible worlds—in a country ruled by nepotism, corruption, and violence. His slogan was broadcast on the radio throughout the day: *"If other countries have oil, gold, or diamonds, Rwanda has peace and national unity."*

In the meantime, segregation prevailed throughout Rwanda. Even foreign aid workers, NGOs, and businesses that employed a large number of Tutsis discretely obeyed the order to respect ethnic and regional balance. Although the Tutsis and certain people from the south of the country denounced ethnic and regional injustices, their cries of alarm were ignored outside of Rwanda.

With the international community, Habyarimana played the game shrewdly and with insight. He never missed an occasion to demonstrate his Catholic faith at the St. Michel Church in Kigali, in Amohoro Stadium, and even in Brussels at the Royal Chapel in the company of the fervently Christian king of the Belgians, Baudoin I. He received unconditional support from the Christian Democrats and made himself into a model member of the Catholic Church in Rwanda. He also cultivated a close friendship with François Mitterand, president of France, not on the basis of Christian faith, but on the basis of the business relationship between their two sons. Jean-Christophe Mitterand and Jean-Pierre Habyarimana made money out of illegal industries such as drug sales, gorilla poaching, and prostitution.[23]

The wide support that Habyarimana enjoyed abroad made it nearly impossible for human rights groups to focus public attention on blatant ethnic segregation of Tutsis; regional discrimination against southerners; the dead bodies at Ruhengeri prison; the shadows of Kigali prison; torture and murders by the secret service; the electric chair at the president's palace; the massacres of Bagogwe;[24] the extermination of the herders of Mutara; the pogroms against the Tutsis of Bugesera, Kibirira, Kibuye, and Murambi; the assassination of journalists and members of the political opposition; the mines planted at primary schools, in taxis, and in other public places; the murder of newborn babies in hospitals; and all the macabre events that amounted to a prelude to the genocide.

An Intellectual Genocide

The intellectual foundations of the genocide are described in *The Rapport Between Education and Employment in Black Africa*,[25] which presents the following arguments:

> Belgian educational policy was characterized by a utilitarian and religious orientation that was called "Belgian paternalism." It was focused on the practical benefits of education, attaching little importance to studies that did not lead directly to improvement in productivity and the economic needs of the metropole.[26]
>
> At the moment of Independence, 1 July 1962, Rwanda had only a superficial primary education system. The majority of secondary schools were still in the start-up phase.[27] Secondary schools in Rwanda did not yet have a complete European program in humanities. Many years would pass before the first students received their diplomas from the secondary schools of Kigali and Nyanza, from the scientific program at Astrida or from the Girls' School of Gisenyi.[28]

Before independence there was no university in Rwanda. Only a select few Rwandan students attended foreign universities such as the

University of Lovanium (Kinshasa) and the University at Elizabethville (Lubumbashi), both in Zaire.

It was in this context of a profound lack of intellectual resources that Rwanda became independent and implemented a system of ethnic quotas. At the same time that all the other countries of Africa were moving ahead with the training of mid- and high-level civil servants, the regime of President Kayibanda exacerbated Rwanda's existing lack of trained civil servants through policies of quotas and ethnic segregation.

Not satisfied with limiting Tutsi intellectuals by the quota system, the government of the First Republic began to massacre Tutsis. This qualified as intellectual genocide.

> The massacre of Tutsis by Hutus in Rwanda was aimed above all
> at the systematic elimination of the actual and future elite of the
> tribe and reached the mass of Tutsis only as a ricochet.[29]

While the First Republic targeted only one ethnic group, the Tutsis, the Second Republic extended its policy of segregation to include the Hutu family members of the politicians and dignitaries of the previous government. Discrimination was focused not only on the Tutsis, but on anyone opposed to the Habyarimana regime. In this spirit, the government of the Second Republic instituted its policy of ethnic and regional equilibrium.

Despite the odious nature of this policy, certain supporters of the government, in their intellectual myopia, attempted to justify this equilibrium. Such was the case of Emmanuel Ndagijimana in his article titled *"The Dynamic of Ethnic and Regional Equilibrium in Rwandan Secondary Schooling,"* which attempted to explain the rationale for this policy.[30]

Their error in judgment was such that even university professors prostituted their talents and their writings. Professor Laurien Uwizeyimana found, through manipulating figures, that

> [O]ne can say . . . that no region or ethnic group is systematically
> excluded, at least at the level of employment, as the *Inkotanyi*
> (Tutsis) have confirmed. Rwanda does not practice any form of
> segregation that could justify aggression, if one accepts that the

country must share equitably the little that it possesses. We believe that we have demonstrated this clearly.[31]

Another group of intellectuals and professors from the University of Ruhengeri, organized around Vice-Rector Anatole Rwagasana, among them François Xavier Bangamwabo, Maniragaba Baributsa, Eustache Munyantwali, Jean Damascene Nduwayezu, Antoine Nyagaheme, Emmanuel Rukiramakuba, Jean Gualbert Rumiya, and Laurien Uwizeyimana, wrote, during the middle of the war in 1991, a book titled *Interethnic Relations in Rwanda in Light of the Aggression of October 1990.*[32] In this book one can see their contribution to the development of an ideology of racism and to the preparations for the genocide of 1994.

Maniragaba Baributsa, for example, asserted that the people of Rwanda lived in complete peace during the Second Republic and that the only difficulties were because of problems between Hutus and Tutsis. I believe that he would even go so far to assert that the murder of Rwandan politicians by the Second Republic at Ruhengeri and Gisenyi was a response to the Hutu-Tutsi problem and that the *Akazu* and Network Zero were a Tutsi creation!

Eustace Munyantwali argued that social integration is a very difficult task because Rwandan society is characterized by the development of a superiority complex in the Tutsis and an inferiority complex in the Hutus. I would like to ask the eminent psychologists of the world to analyze the foundation of these psychological and pedagogical theories in a country where every population group speaks the same language, shares the same religion, the same history, the same culture, lives on the same hillsides, and has intermarried for centuries.[33]

As for François Xavier Bangamwabo and Emmanuel Rukiramakuba, their writings are as militant as war propaganda and warn all Rwandans of good faith to denounce the enemy through the mass media; that was just another way of stirring up ethnic hatred.

Jean Damascene Nduwayezu, before presenting his analysis of several sociopolitical principles on the reintegration of refugees, argued that the war of October 1990, which was unleashed by a group of Rwandan refugees, had nothing to do with refugees, but rather was provoked by a desire for political power. He emphasized that his principles only apply to refugees who have abandoned the arrogance of a race born to dominate.

I can add to this list of incoherent reasoning, but I limit myself to these few examples. Nonetheless, these intellectuals astound me because they so willingly fell into line with a racist and dictatorial government.

The physical elimination of intellectuals began with the elimination of ideas, an obscurantism that destroyed academic and scientific openness. There was only one pattern of acceptable behavior, and intellectuals had to submit to it or run the risk of unemployment, imprisonment, exile, or assassination. This was the beginning of the intellectual genocide.

What was the role of intellectuals in this system? To clarify the role of intellectuals in the bloody tragedy of Rwanda, I classify them into four basic categories: government ideologues, opportunists, passive supporters, and intellectual opponents of the regime.

1. Government ideologues: The intellectual ideologues of the regime were recruited mainly from circles close to government leaders. Generally they occupied well-paid, high positions, for which they were often unqualified. They defended segregationist policies as "their only hope" and fought against the new criteria of meritocracy.

2. Opportunists: These political weathervanes were ready to jump from one political camp to another in search of personal profit. The government in power knew their weakness and exploited it at precise and opportune moments. They hungered for power and money, and could be seen running from ministry to ministry and from political meetings to popular rallies, passing on any new ideas that they thought would be appreciated by those in power. Sometimes they achieved their goals and sometimes they failed miserably.

3. Passive supporters: This group of intellectuals remained disengaged and without opinion. Because of weak personalities or because the system had so subjugated them, they were dominated by events, preferring to live in anonymous resignation to what went on around them. Generally they were floaters without much to say for themselves.

4. Intellectual opponents: Those intellectuals who resigned their posts for ideological reasons became suspect and were often

neutralized. They fought hard against the first two categories of intellectuals and rejected the third category, which they considered ineffective. The regime was extremely oppressive toward these intellectuals. Some of them preferred to live outside of the country, creating a "brain drain" of Rwandan intellectuals. Those who remained lost their jobs and were the targets of imprisonment, torture, and assassination.

It was the first two categories of intellectuals, the government ideologues and the opportunists, who took an active role in the massacres and the genocide.

Genocide in Rwanda: Planned Massacres

It is not necessary here to provide a daily account of the genocide; it is more important to trace its roots to an alliance between the colonialists and the churches. The beginning of the unpunished massacres can be traced to 1 November 1959, when a group of young Tutsis attacked a Hutu notable, Dominique Mbonyumutwa, as he was leaving a church service in the parish of Byimana.

The next day, the conflagration spread through the Gitarama prefecture and throughout the country, leaving a great number of dead and homeless.

The holocaust of the Tutsis was spread out over two years, 1959 to 1961, and was marked by massacres at the following places and dates:

Gitarama, 2 November 1959
Nyanza, 4 November 1959
Gisenyi, 6 November 1959
Kibuye, 6 November 1959
Ruhengeri, 6 November 1959
Byumba, 7 November 1959
Kigali, 7 November 1959
Butare, 10 November 1959
Cyangugu, 1960
Kibungo, 1961

The aggression in Byimana was not a sufficient pretext to merit the consequences of this series of massacres that cost the lives of thousands of people. They required political manipulation, serious psychological preparation, and a well-established plan. On closer examination, one notices that the beginning of the violence was localized in the home region of the president of PARMEHUTU and future president of the First Republic, Gregoire Kayibanda. It continued in the zones of influence of the leaders of PARMEHUTU, such as Barthazar Bicamumpaka in Ruhengeri and Callixte Habamenshi in Gisenyi.

Soon after taking power, the racist government began its campaign to gradually eliminate the Tutsis. Here are some of the most notable dates:

October 1961, massacre of Tutsis in the Byumba prefecture.

1 December 1962, execution at Ruhengeri of 14 young Tutsis suspected of being Inyenzi terrorists after a summary trial.

4 July 1962, 100 young Tutsis executed at Ruhengeri.

24 December 1962, execution at Ruhengeri of all opposition party leaders.

1 January 1964, Tutsis were made to run a gauntlet of machetes, their houses burned and their cattle killed.

November 1966, massive arrest of Tutsis without regard for sex or age, and summary executions at Cyangugu, Gisenyi, and Kibungo. Each time the pretext for the killings was an attack by Inyenzi rebels.

February 1973, Tutsis scapegoated by a tired president, by a regime on its last legs, and by a coup plotted by soldiers from the north of Rwanda.

1 October 1990, attack by the RPF from Uganda.

2 October–20 November 1990, massive arrests of more than 10,000 Tutsis and members of opposition parties.

January–March 1991, massacres of the Bagogwe Tutsis in the northwest of Rwanda and Tutsi herders in the northeast.

February–March 1992, massacres of Tutsis in the region of Bugesera and in the prefecture of Kigali.

22 and 23 February 1994, assassinations of Felicien Gatabazi, minister of public works, and of Martin Bucyana, president of the CDR (a Hutu extremist party) and generalized massacres throughout almost all of Rwanda.

From March 1994, sporadic and unpunished massacres throughout the country. Tutsis began to seek shelter in

churches, convents, and monasteries as well as in local
government offices.

6 April 1994, the terrible news of the death of the presidents of
Rwanda and Burundi is broadcast on the radio. Barricades
are erected, and the hunt for Tutsis and Hutu opposition
members begins across the country with the help of lists
prepared in advance.

April–July 1994, orders issued to "spare no one, all Tutsis must
die." Soldiers, militias, and the population take part in a
massive butchery.

The panacea for all the ills of the Kayibanda regime was a perpetual series of pogroms against the Tutsis. The first attacks were principally focused on Tutsi intellectuals, priests, monks, nuns, secondary and university students, and bureaucrats. Although the killings began as a liquidation of Tutsi intellectuals, later even Tutsi peasants were not spared.

In 1990, on the campus of the National University in Ruhengeri, a media campaign was launched by highly placed officials at the school, with the complicity of university officials at the national level, to identify Tutsis wherever they were. Many teachers, school officials, and students at the National University were arrested and imprisoned.

To conclude, one cannot talk of freedom in Rwanda without speaking of the country's previous political, administrative, and religious systems and the roles they played in the events that led to so much bloodshed. The segregationist heritage of the colonialists, implemented through the colonial administration and schools, that first favored the Tutsis, then the Hutus, bore its fruit during the genocide. The principle of "divide and conquer," used by the colonialists and certain members of the churches in Rwanda, served its purpose. In Rwanda, violent opposition of one ethnic group to another became an instrument of transition through difficult political and economic periods.

Instead of working against segregationist policy, the governments that succeeded the colonial administration sought to perpetuate it. The racism of the ethnic state violated basic human rights and liberties in all domains. From the violation of basic liberties, the institutions of the state turned to the planning and execution of genocide.

■ FRANÇOIS BYARAHAMUWANZI, DIRECTOR, HUMAN RIGHTS LEAGUE OF THE GREAT LAKES REGION, RWANDAN ASSOCIATION FOR THE DEFENSE OF HUMAN RIGHTS

We have already heard about some of the experiences of my fellow countrymen who lived through the massacres, and some analysis of the historical and sociocultural basis of the genocide. I would like to add to these perspectives my experience as a human rights activist who lived through the same events.

I will start by saying that Rwandan human rights organizations were particularly active in denouncing the events that led up to the genocide. In 1990, we were among the first to say that genocide was taking place in Rwanda. We denounced the genocide in declarations, articles, and reports that we submitted to our partner organizations in the international community. The international community was aware of the situation in Rwanda. In cooperation with the opposition political parties, we fought the dictatorship, to the point that we were considered to be in the first line of the opposition to the former regime. Some people in this first line of opposition—many of us in fact—paid for this with their lives.

We called for an international investigation into the massacres of the Bagogwe people and those at Bugesera, an investigation that attracted worldwide attention. More recently, just after returning from exile, we organized an investigation into the organization of the genocide, beginning in Kigali. We will soon broaden our investigations to include the entire country.

What is remarkable is that one finds people of all sorts among the organizers of the genocide—intellectuals, businessmen, farm workers, bureaucrats, soldiers, priests and nuns. Every socio-professional category was implicated in the genocide.

What happened here was genocide. I don't say this because it is evident to everyone, but because I have already heard people, both here and abroad, who deny that it was genocide, who speak of it in other terms. Without going into the academic definition of genocide, I say that this was a true genocide because all Tutsis were to be killed. The Tutsis in Rwanda who are alive today owe their lives to chance, to luck. They simply did not run into a killer. They hid themselves.

Although many Hutus were killed, more than you would think, there was always a reason for their deaths. In each case, there was an explanation. Hutus were killed because they were involved with the political opposition, because they were human rights activists, because they were married to Tutsi women, because they were educated, because they were rich. All of these were reasons for their death. The Tutsis were killed only because they were Tutsis. This is what is called genocide.

The genocide in Rwanda was prepared in minute detail. I will not repeat the proof that you have read elsewhere, but the proof is demonstrated first in the rapidity with which the massacres took place. One minute after the president's plane crashed, the massacres started. In certain places, the massacres began even before the plane crashed. There were places in the countryside, as in the commune of Satché in the Kibungo prefecture, where the massacres started the day before. Everything was known in advance. The plane crashed at around 8:20 P.M. local time, and moments after the crash, we saw bureaucrats, people like us, with whom we had shared a beer just an hour before, with military weapons. They had already started the killings. This means that they received their weapons beforehand. This means that they learned how to use them beforehand. This is more proof that the organization of the genocide was planned in advance in minute detail.

The genocide was not ethnic, contrary to what some people want to believe; it was political. In reality, the organizers of the genocide, the people in power at the time, thought and said that by killing the Tutsis they would win the war. Why? Because in their little heads, they believed that the RPF fought only for the Tutsis, even though the RPF said to anyone who would listen that they were not fighting for the Tutsis, they were fighting for Rwanda. The extremists didn't want to hear anything else; they were convinced that the RPF was fighting for the Tutsis. Therefore they thought that in killing the Tutsis inside Rwanda they would eliminate the accomplices of the RPF, discouraging them and taking away their reason for fighting, forcing them to accept the conditions imposed on them—this was the Habyarimana version of the Arusha Accords. It was a very simple, but very serious, error in analysis that cost more than one million lives. It also had a boomerang effect on the organizers of the genocide who are now in Zaire.

Another thing that proves that the genocide was political, not ethnic, is that, contrary to what people think, not all Hutus in Rwanda participated in the genocide. Not every Hutu is guilty of killing Tutsis.

Most of the organizers, the instigators, and the executioners were Hutus, but among their ranks there were also Tutsis. (The leader of the *Interahamwe* youth wing is a Tutsi by birth.) The Hutus who organized this genocide were extremists coerced or manipulated by politicians. It must be understood that this was not a simple affair of Hutu against Tutsi.

Since April 1994, the world has talked about "the genocide," but in reality the international community makes distinctions among three types of crimes: genocide, political crimes, and war crimes. We cannot neglect the last two, which were also committed in Rwanda. The crime of genocide in Rwanda is well known: It was the murder of the Tutsis simply because they were Tutsis. Political crimes involved killing people because of their political beliefs, most of whom were Hutus considered to be supporters of the Tutsis or members of the opposition. There were also Tutsis who were killed because of their political beliefs, or because the people who killed them thought that they were members of the opposition. Members of opposition parties and diverse opposition organizations were all victims of political crimes. There were also war crimes, when soldiers killed civilians or prisoners of war. Only God knows how many civilians were killed by the military—not because they were Tutsis, but just because they were in the wrong place at the wrong time. Tens of thousands of civilians were killed by the military. They cannot be forgotten.

Futhermore, one cannot generalize and say that everyone who participated in the genocide has the same level of responsibility. First there are the instigators of the genocide, those who conceived of committing genocide to achieve their political goals. In reality, a very small group of people were associated with the government and were members of the *Akazu* or inner circle of President Habyarimana. These members of the *Akazu* were the instigators of, and bear primary responsibility for, the genocide.

Second, there were the organizers of the genocide, the people who since 1990 met over and over again to discuss and to plan their tactics for committing genocide. Many people knew where they met and what they talked about. Many human rights organizations denounced these meetings and made it public knowledge that these meetings were taking place. The organizers included high-ranking bureaucrats, officials from different political parties—notably the MRND, the MDR,[34] and the CDR—military officers, prefects, subprefects, *bourgmestres*, members of the Church, bishops, priests, and others. People sometimes ask why the Tutsis didn't flee, since the organizers of the genocide were meeting openly. It has been asserted that people did not flee because they trusted these high-ranking members of society, and yet these very people were the organizers of the genocide.

Third, there were the executioners. These were the unfortunate people who picked up their machetes, clubs, or guns to kill, at times not knowing why they were doing it. I am sure that the day these people are arrested, when they are asked why they did it, some of them will not be able to give an answer. The instigators and the organizers will always be able to go into long Hitlerian speeches to explain why the Tutsis had to die. They have already written about this.[35]

Finally, there were the accomplices of the genocide. These were the well-known people who denounced others, who pointed the finger at others. They were not always visible, more often they were behind the scenes, but there were many of them. They will be very difficult to find because they are the kind of people who tend to stay in the shadows.

Among the organizers and even the executioners of the genocide we have found a large number of so-called intellectuals. It is better perhaps to call them people who have had an education. Their complicity went so far that one must wonder why Rwandans even go to university. It is truly astonishing to see an engineer take up a machete and slit the throat of his neighbor for no reason, to kill without motive. We know who these people are. I believe that the educated people of Rwanda who participated in the genocide and its organization should be ashamed. I believe, in response to the genocide, that Rwanda needs to take a serious look at the educational system, because what has been taught to our children up to this point is worthless.

Until now, everyone who speaks of genocide blames the Rwandan people as a whole, as if all Rwandans participated in the genocide and in the massacres. This is not true. I will give you three examples of categories of people who played a very positive role during the genocide.

First, I congratulate the courage of the soldiers of the Rwandan Patriotic Army (RPA). I would like to relate an experience that I lived through, because I am one of the people who was saved by this army. While the RPA was involved in violent battles in Kigali, they saved the lives of people who did not even call them for help. On 2 May 1994, at midnight, soldiers of the RPA jumped over the wall at my house and took me and all my neighbors to safety. They did the same thing at least 10 times in my neighborhood. While they were risking their lives to save me and my neighbors, 68 people had just been killed in the fighting. Each day hundreds of bombs whistled over my house, and amid the worst of the fighting the RPA came to rescue us, risking their own lives. When they came to take us away at midnight, they took us on foot to their camp at Rebero Horizon, where we arrived at 3:00 A.M. We stayed there two days, and then they took us to Remera. Three days later they took us to Byumba. These were people like you and me, who had families, who risked their lives to save others. An RPA lieutenant and a colonel came several times, risking death, to save people in my neighborhood.

The second example is the many Rwandans, most of them Hutus, who risked their lives to save Tutsis. Only the Hutus could save Tutsis, and we must recognize those Hutus who risked their lives to save their neighbors. Most of them were killed for their bravery and beliefs. They were executed along with the people they tried to save.

The third example is those expatriates who stayed on in Rwanda and saved lives. Two are Father Richard, a Frenchman, and Father Otto, a German, who worked at the Saint André School. These two men saved dozens of people at the risk of their own lives. One of them was shot in the arm. In the countryside there were nuns, doctors, and aid workers who risked their lives to save Rwandans. I want to emphasize this because everyone always talks about the flight of the expatriates, about how UNAMIR, the United Nations, diplomats, and aid workers ran from danger, but people don't talk enough about those who stayed, those who left and took Rwandans with them, or those who risked their lives to save Rwandans.

I want to emphasize the importance of judging the guilty. There are both a national and an international criminal tribunal to prosecute those who are guilty of genocide. These tribunals are important because everyone talks of "national reconciliation," but reconciliation must begin with the punishment of the guilty. If there is but one person guilty of genocide who goes unpunished in this country, reconciliation will be impossible. We ask you to help the Rwandan people to organize fair trials for the genocide; all criminals must be tried without distinction.

Several perplexing issues have arisen from the genocide. First, what about the "innocent criminals?" Who are these innocent criminals? They are the people who were forced to kill; in some cases they were forced to kill their own families, in exchange for their lives. There is an ongoing debate about the people who say they were required to kill. Can we agree with this idea? Is a criminal not a criminal? Can one be forced to kill? And if one is forced to kill, is one innocent or not?

Rwanda has again brought up the question of the right of intervention. Does a country have the right to intervene in another country in order to save lives? An example of this is the situation in Burundi, where everything is in place to carry out massacres very similar to the ones that took place in Rwanda. The Burundian press incites violence, just like the press in Rwanda. There are Hutu and Tutsi militias in Burundi, the same as in Rwanda. Everyone knows about the preparations for massacres. There are extremist politicians. The civilian population is being armed. No one knows how many civilians have guns, but there are some who even have silencers, who execute people at cafés in full daylight. Everyone sees this, but what is being done? Nothing. Will the Burundians and the international community wait for more massacres to take place in order to respond? I use this digression to make a point, that the international community sometimes hides behind international law in order to refuse to intervene in time to save human lives. The question I pose is, should the right of intervention exist?

Can what happened in Rwanda happen again in the next 10 years? I think it can. What happened in Rwanda was, first, a question of power, a political affair. If we do not maintain a vigilant eye on government, genocide can recur. The Rwandan people and the international community must keep an eye on the politicians. It is also important to look closely at education and at what is being taught to the population. We were astonished to see how readily the people of Rwanda responded to the government call to kill their neighbors. What was the reason for this? Poor education and a largely illiterate population. Has anything been done to improve this situation? I invite you to help us to educate the children of Rwanda and reeducate the population. If the people are not reeducated and virulent politicians take over again, there will be more massacres in Rwanda.

■ MAJOR FRANK RUSAGARA, PUBLIC AFFAIRS OFFICER,
RWANDAN PATRIOTIC ARMY

I want to emphasize the fact that Rwanda is one of the oldest nation
states in Africa, with a common language and a common culture
among all its peoples. When the first colonialists came, they could not
believe that there was only one people and that all these people came
from Rwanda. The colonialists then distorted Rwanda's history by saying that the Tutsi people must be from North Africa. This was an intentional confusion of issues. The colonialists did not believe that
Rwandans could have achieved their own nation state, that Africans
were capable of this. Therefore these people must have descended from
the Hamites; they were not Africans.

Before colonialism, Rwanda had many great achievements as a
nation. The country was well organized, with a developed political
structure. Because of its strong army, Rwanda was able to escape the
slave traders. Rwandan society was very coherent, having succeeded in
achieving its own unity, its own nation state. When the colonialists
arrived, Rwandan society was cohesive but was also still evolving.

Upon their arrival in Rwanda, both the German and Belgian colonialists used standard divide-and-conquer policies. They saw an advantage in emphasizing the differences and dividing the people of Rwanda
rather than focusing on the similarities all Rwandans shared. The Tutsis
were favored by the colonialists and were given education and jobs in
the administration. They also were made responsible for organizing
forced labor, collecting taxes, etc. Some historians have made it seem
that this system of forced labor was a Tutsi invention, not a part of the
colonial system. This deliberate distortion of history was taught to
young children in school and was even believed by some Rwandans.

I have known Rwandan Tutsis who suffered under colonial rule at
the hands of other Tutsis, who were ordered to perform forced labor by
the Tutsi agents of colonialist rule. In the arid areas where there were
many cattle and therefore many Tutsis, the colonialists had fewer
Hutus to subject to forced labor, so in those areas, and in others, Tutsis
were made to work like their Hutu brothers and sisters. They were
made to cultivate cash crops, build roads, or dig irrigation ditches.
Many of the Tutsis in these areas fled across the borders to Uganda and
Tanzania. In fact, many of those Tutsi who left in 1959 fled the country
not because of the pogroms that began then, but because they had suf-

fered at the hands of Tutsis under colonial rule. Colonialism was not selective, but it was very thorough. It was not only Hutus who bore the brunt of colonialism, but all of the peasant class, Tutsi peasants included.

Before 1959, the Belgians favored the Tutsis, but just before independence they changed their alliance. The Hutus became the favored group and were given education, jobs in administration, etc. With the formation of the PARMEHUTU party, emancipation of the Hutus led the political agenda. The Belgians sought partnership with radical Hutus who traded Rwanda's independence for Hutu emancipation. There was an emphasis on emancipation and a feeling that independence could be delayed. Because of this, sectarian politics were the foundation of the First Republic. The situation at the time was strongly influenced by the Belgians, who saw it in their interest to keep Rwanda in their grip, and who forced the issues of Hutu emancipation and social revolution over independence.

The origins of the social revolution of 1959 did not come from within Rwandan society. Emancipation was not in the national interest as it meant inclusion for one group of people, the Hutus, and exclusion and banishment for another group, the Tutsis. It was the denial of the sovereign right of nationality to one group of Rwandans as part of this so-called social revolution that laid the foundation for the genocide. Emancipation of the Hutus meant denial of the rights of other non-Hutu Rwandans.

Although Gregoire Kayibanda, the first president of this country, was not a scholar, he had powerful advisors who convinced him that this lowering of the Tutsis in order to build up the Hutus was a great national feat, that the choice of Hutu emancipation over Rwandan independence would bring him fame as a leader.

What has passed for politics in Rwanda, what the politicians have done to this country, was a big lie. Yet there are still people who talk about the emancipation of the Hutus. For the last 36 years Rwandan Hutus have been told by their politicians that "we are working for your emancipation." Have the Hutus been emancipated? They have been working at this for 36 years, and what does Rwanda have to show for it? This is why I call this the Era of the Big Lie.

The politicians of the First and Second Republics expected the people of Rwanda to devote themselves to "the cause," to kill Tutsis year in and year out, to vote only for the extremist candidates, to wear party colors, all in the name of the emancipation of the Hutus. Have the Hutus, the majority of the Rwandan people, really been emancipated? The population has gone along with its leaders. The people have accepted the lie as truth, they have killed, they have participated actively in genocide, all in the name of emancipation. This is the big lie.

My office is in the Ministry of Defense, and I recently found the job description for the person in my position in the former government. One of the responsibilities listed in this job description was to mobilize the population *vis à vis animation*. The word *animation* in French means to inflame or impassion the population—I assume, in this case, with some form of political propaganda. The person who was in my position got people to sing empty slogans day in and day out, overworking himself not by talking about programs or educating the people about the realities of life in Rwanda, but by teaching propaganda and promising emancipation.

Immediately after the Referendum of Independence of 1959, thousands of people were killed and thousands more were banished and exiled. No one in Rwanda dared to say anything about this, and little was written in the international community. When the journalists did write about Rwanda, the only thing that was said was how backward the Africans were, busy killing one another in yet another "tribal war." Why was it that when the Europeans first arrived they saw Rwanda as an advanced society and claimed that a political system like the one developed in Rwanda had to be imported? It seems that contact with the Europeans and the colonial experience changed Rwandans. Once they gained independence they started butchering each other; they started killing one another as they never had before.

The politicians of the First Republic distorted the history of this country. You meet people who talk about the history of Rwanda and who fail to articulate its achievements. They base their understanding of history on the revisionist version instead of being proud of their true history.

The former government created a climate of fear by saying that the Tutsis could come and invade the country at any time, to kill the Hutus' families, to change the fabric of Rwandan society. The scare was deliberate, a part of government policy. It was common to tell children when they were bad that the RPF would come to take them away to use them as slaves. People were conditioned to fear and hate the Tutsis from birth.

But it was Rwandan academics who rewrote history and taught this history to the people of Rwanda. I once heard a Rwandan Hutu academic address a group of people on the topic of the experience of the Rwandan people—about how the Tutsis oppressed the Hutus. He began his presentation by saying that the Tutsis made a practice of castrating all Hutu men and then using their testicles to decorate the ceremonial Tutsi drums. When this statement was questioned by someone in the audience, he went further, to say that this was systematically done to the Hutu population. How is it, then, that the Hutus came to be the majority? The people of Rwanda came to believe that these lies were the truth because of the revisionist history put forward by academics and used by politicians to their own benefit.

Another revisionist distortion put forward by academics is that democracy existed in colonial and postcolonial Rwanda. The colonists credit themselves with having organized democratic elections, and with bringing about Rwandan independence. It is true that elections were held in Rwanda, but were they a democratic expression of the Rwandan people? When Rwandans went to vote, did they really vote for ideas or programs advanced by politicians, or did they vote Hutu or Tutsi, or Twa for that matter? Many Rwandans were uneducated or so naive that they voted for colors. They voted "red" or "green," following the colors of the extremist groups.

The international community, in the past, held up Rwanda as the African model of democracy, a democratic country that held fair elections. They said that thanks to the great stability created by the Kayibanda and Habyarimana regimes, elections were held, and therefore the people of Rwanda had a voice. But were the elections representative and democratic? People in Rwanda did not vote for candidates because of what they stood for or their ideas, but rather Rwandans voted for candidates based on their "tribal" affiliation, on whether they were born Hutu or Tutsi. Ethnicity had become so institutionalized that even politicians who had good ideas and were trained and educated lost because they were not Hutus. Does the international community call these democratic elections? In my opinion this is barely even a census—just a counting by tribal affiliation.

This was another part of the big lie. You can link it back to the colonial polarization of the Rwandan people into the artificial racial classifications the Belgians imposed in the 1930s. Failing to achieve absolute division in Rwandan society, the colonialists started to base racial classification on the number of cows you owned. If you owned less than 10 cows, you were a Hutu; if you owned 10 or more, you were a Tutsi. In fact, some of us may be Tutsis because our grandfathers borrowed a cow and some may be Hutus because our grandfathers slaughtered a cow the day before the census.[36]

Before colonialism, there was mobility in Rwandan society; a Hutu could become a Tutsi, or a Tutsi a Hutu, the two groups were so intertwined. There were many "mixed" marriages between Hutus and Tutsis. Defining people's supposed "racial identity," as the former government would have put it, was actually one of the biggest challenges for the colonial administration.

I am convinced that I am a Tutsi, because my father and my family left Rwanda in 1961 just after the revolution, when I was very young. While I was in exile I had relatives who were still here in Rwanda. To illustrate the complexity of the situation in Rwanda, one of my female relatives, my cousin, was married to a Hutu. When the killing started in April, her husband was killed. They had hidden separately because my cousin was a Tutsi and her husband, fearing that she would attract attention to their children and himself, took their five children to his brother's house, leaving her to hide in the bush. The husband's brother was not a targeted Hutu; he was an extremist, an *Interahamwe*. He knew that his sister-in-law, my cousin, was a Tutsi and because of this he killed his own brother and his nieces and nephews who were all Hutus. But my cousin stayed hidden in the bush and survived. When she told me about her ordeal, I asked her, "How could this happen? Your Hutu husband and your children were killed by your brother-in-law for no reason other than your ethnic identity." The brother-in-law was arrested and is now in Kigali prison.

The situation in Rwanda is very complicated and difficult to figure out. It will not be easy to point out who did what to whom in Rwanda. There was a genocide, but the government also killed many people who were not Tutsis. With so much intermarriage, it was just too difficult to tell who was who, so if you had a Tutsi identity card you died, or if you looked like a Tutsi you died.

Many politicians who used fear of the Tutsis to mobilize the Hutus were themselves married to Tutsis. Many of the extremist Hutu politicians had no fundamental quarrel with the Tutsis. If they had, how would they have allowed themselves to marry Tutsis? Their offspring were Tutsis or at least had Tutsi blood. It was only when they left their bedrooms and their homes that they would attack the Tutsis.

Not every Hutu was as fundamentally racist as the former government would like people to think. Many of the anti-Tutsi sentiments expressed by Hutu extremists were voiced only for effect, to improve their political position and to ingratiate themselves with the government. If these expressions of racism and separatism had been a reality, they would not have been able to stomach having a Tutsi in their own home or in their bedroom. There was even intermarriage on the part of government officials, despite government policy clearly stating that no official in the Habyarimana government would be allowed to marry an *Inyenzi*, a Tutsi. This is typical of how the Second Republic was a government of hypocrisy and lies.

It is important for the world to understand the complexity of the situation in Rwanda in order to provide assistance. It is also important as a catalyst to change the way that the humanitarian and international communities conduct themselves and how they deal with this type of crisis in the future. Postindependence politics, to a great extent, laid the framework for the genocide. Hatred was institutionalized. The international community must try to understand the politics of Rwanda without being influenced by the propaganda of the former government.

Rwanda in the time of Habyarimana was among the world's highest recipients of development assistance per capita. The international community felt that in giving money to Rwanda they were supporting democracy in Africa. The Swiss were here, the Germans, the Belgians, the Americans, the French, everybody was here. They were supporting democracy and holding up Rwanda as a model of democratic multiparty rule. Habyarimana fooled the world with the "big lie," and look at what has happened to this "model of democracy." The politicians of this country used the political paralysis of the people of Rwanda to expand the culture of impunity for their own advancement, for their own political ends. They saw the benefit of pitting segments of the population against each other in the name of democracy. Can the international community, in the name of international solidarity, be proud of what took place here?

The politics of this country over the last 35 years should be reconsidered, and each donor country should reassess its own involvement. Members of the international community should not claim naïveté; they have a responsibility to be aware of the world around them, to know what is happening in the countries in which they work. And each individual has the responsibility to be aware, before entering a country, of that country's history. Every humanitarian or development worker should be trained before coming to give away food or plant trees in a foreign country.

Help us to forge unity and to focus on the common values that we have shared for 500 years. Help us to reeducate our people, to teach them the values that we shared before colonialism. There are of course differences—dances, hairstyles, and other cultural variations—but these are not fundamental. What is fundamental is that there is a common language and that we have no real quarrel with each other.

There have been suggestions of demarcating Rwanda, of making one country for Hutus and another for Tutsis. Perhaps this is what the French had in mind when they came and established the *Zone Turquoise*.[37] This is preposterous and it simply won't work. This suggestion may have found support with the former government, the perpetrators of the genocide who thought they could exterminate the Tutsis and all of the opposition; perhaps they would have accepted having a separate Hutu nation. You must remember that for 500 years the Tutsis and the Hutus have lived together and have shared this land. You simply cannot turn the clock back 500 years.

Notes

1. A good attempt to explain poverty and its relation to violence is presented in the last chapter of *Rwanda, appauvrissement et ajustement structurel* (Bruxelles: Cahier Africains, 1995), p. 81.

2. Traditional historian of the court. All of the history of Rwanda was related orally and was passed on in this manner from one *Abiru* to the next.

3. See Gérard Prunier, "La crise Rwandaise," *Refugee Survey Quarterly*, 1994.

4. During the genocide, massacres often took place over the course of several days, with the killers coming back again and again to take care of the "work" they had not finished the day before.

5. Published in *Kangura* in December 1990. See Chapter 4 for the full text.

6. Before the genocide of 1994, churches were considered to be safe havens where Tutsis and members of the opposition could seek refuge and receive sanctuary. The genocide of 1994 brought about the first widespread "violation" of the churches. This use of the church as a safe haven was known to the former government and used to its advantage in the organization of the genocide (see Chapter 4). There were also instances where members of the clergy, nuns, and priests participated in the massacres (see Chapter 6).

7. Conference held in Berlin to divide Africa among the European colonial powers and establish spheres of influence on the African continent.

8. Rwandan monarch. *Mwami*, or God-King, was believed to have been sent by God to act as the intermediary between God and the Rwandan people.

9. See P. Erny, *De l'education traditionnelle à l'enseignement moderne au Rwanda 1900–1975* (Lille: Université de Lille III, 1981), p. 55.

10. Ibid., p. 66.

11. The first president of Rwanda, the former editor-in-chief of the missionary newspaper *Kinymateka*, and a protegé of Perraudin.

12. Fidele Nkundabagenzi, *Rwanda Politique 1958–1960*. (Bruxelles: CRISP, 1961), p. 20.

13. Platform of PARMEHUTU, the "Hutu Manifesto" outlined a segregationist policy of Hutu emancipation through ethnic quotas.

14. PARMEHUTU was also the party of President Kayibanda. It used Hutu emancipation as its platform and promoted the ideas outlined in the Bahutu Manifesto.

15. Nkundabagenzi, op. cit., p. 119.

16. See Collette Braeckman, *Rwanda: Histoire d'un génocide* (Paris: Librairie Artheme Fayard, 1994), p. 83.

17. Ibid., p. 51.

18. Ibid., p. 52.

19. Léon Mugesera is currently wanted by the International Criminal Tribunal for Rwanda for crimes against humanity. He is per-

haps most famous for his speech during an MRND party rally on 22 November 1992 when he proposed the following solution to the problem of Tutsi "cockroaches" and accomplices: "They belong in Ethiopia and we are going to find them a short-cut to get there by throwing them in the Nyabarongo river [that flows north]. I must insist on this point. We have to act. Wipe them all out!" (See Fédération Internationale des Droits de l'Homme, *Report of the Commission of Inquiry on Human Rights Violations in Rwanda,* pp. 24–25.)

20. Period from 1973 until 1994. The Second Republic was dominated by MRND, the party of President Juvenal Habyarimana.

21. Kinyarwanda for "small hut" is a pejorative term for people of the same family who share the privileges and the wealth of the country among themselves to the exclusion of all others. See also Braeckman, *Rwanda: Histoire d'un genocide,* p. 104.

22. A group of extremists close to the president who planned and carried out the genocide, many of whose members had close ties to Agathe Kanziga, Habyarimana's wife.

23. See Pascal Krop, *Le génocide Franco-Africain* (Paris: Éditions Jean-Claude Lattès, 1994), p. 11.

24. A massacre of 500 to 1,000 Bagogwe, a Tutsi tribe living in northern Rwanda, that took place in early 1991. This massacre and others were investigated in 1993 by the International Commission of Inquiry, which focused investigations on human rights violations in Rwanda since 1 October 1990. Its report was published on 8 March 1993.

25. Jean Damascène Ndyambaje, *Rapports entre l'éducation et l'emploi en Afrique noire* (Fribourg: Éditions St. Paul, 1995).

26. Ibid., p. 90.

27. Ibid., p. 187.

28. Ibid.

29. See L. Sylla, *Tribalisme et parti unique en Afrique noire* (Paris: Presse de la Fondation Nationale des Sciences, 1977), pp. 320–21.

30. See Emmanuel Ndagijimana, *Dynamique des équilibres ethnique et régional dans l'enseignement secondaire Rwandais* (Kigali: Ministère de l'Enseignement Primaire et Secondaire, 1986).

31. See Laurien Uwizeyimana, "Ethnic and Regional Equilibrium in Employment," *Dialogue* 146 (May–June 1991): p. 31.

32. Discussed by F. X. Bangamwabo and colleagues in *Les relations interethniques au Rwanda à la lumière de l'agression d'octobre 1990* (Ruhengeri: Édition Universitaire du Rwanda, 1991).

33. For an alternative viewpoint on this inferiority/superiority complex and its role in the genocide, see Gérard Prunier, *The Rwanda Crisis: History of a Genocide* (London: Hurst and Co., 1995).

34. *Mouvement Démocratique Républicain*, one of the principal opposition parties.

35. See "The Rwandan People Accuse . . .," Chapter 4.

36. The Belgians were faced with a dilemma in their racial classification system when, at the home of the grandson of the *mwami*, they found that he did not own the required 10 cows. He was nonetheless classified as a Tutsi.

37. The French army returned to Rwanda in June 1994, with the approval of the UN Security Council, to establish the *Zone Turquoise*, a "humanitarian safe zone" in southwestern Rwanda. The French safe zone was not intended to stop the genocide, as it was established in areas still under control of the Rwandan Armed Forces (FAR), which continued to systematically murder Tutsis. Although by this time the extent of the genocide had become known, the French refused to arrest or allow the arrest of the organizers of the genocide among members of the former government and the FAR while they were in the *Zone Turquoise*, effectively allowing them to escape to Zaire.

UNITY AND DIVISION

Introduction

■ **JOHN A. BERRY AND CAROL POTT BERRY**

Since the early 20th century, Rwandan society has been both unified and divided by the influences of racism, political struggle, demographic pressure, and foreign intervention. Though each of these factors was discussed in turn by various speakers, none can be considered the unique cause of the genocide. It is more relevant to consider how each contributed in its own way to the genocide.

It has been argued that the conflict in Rwanda is not ethnically based as Hutus and Tutsis share the same language, religion, and traditions. However, since colonial times racism, violence, and separatism have been inescapable elements of Rwandan political culture. Racial divisions in Rwanda were cemented by the Belgians in the mid-1930s with the imposition of an identity card system specifying the bearer's racial group, but it was the post-independence governments of the First and Second Republics that ruthlessly exploited these divisions for their own political ends. Rwandan progressives regard the conflict inherent in the Rwandan political system not as one between the Hutus and the Tutsis, but one between the government and the people of Rwanda.

Although some academics point to the demographic roots of the Rwandan genocide, their arguments often ignore the role of the government and of the people of Rwanda in the genocide. Rwanda is still the most densely populated country in Africa, but overpopulation does not, in and of itself, lead to organized mass murder. No government, even that of an overpopulated country like Rwanda, would perpetrate genocide if it regarded all of its people as a resource to be cultivated rather than some of its people as a threat to be exterminated.

The international community also contributed in numerous ways to creating and sustaining an environment in which genocide could occur. For decades, Western donors supported the Rwandan government's practice of racial violence and separatist politics by providing foreign aid. (In addition to having the highest population density in Africa, it was sometimes joked that Rwanda had the highest density of foreign aid workers on the continent.) But the West refused to recognize the political and racial dimensions of the violence in Rwanda even after it was reported by reputable sources. When finally faced with the overwhelming evidence that genocide was taking place, the Western powers[1] did not mobilize to act until after the killings were over, the exodus of refugees had begun, and cholera had broken out in the refugee camps.

The following chapter examines each of these contributing factors from the point of view of a journalist, an aid worker, a doctor, and a soldier. All of the speakers are Rwandans reflecting on the strengths and shortcomings that unify and divide their own society.

The Artificial Racialization at the Root of the Rwandan Genocide

▧ **FAUSTIN KAGAME, JOURNALIST**

The discovery in 1945 of the Nazi concentration camps where the "final solution" was applied to Jewish men, women, and children gave rise to a hope that the world would be more vigilant and that any future attempt at Nazification and genocide would be denounced and condemned.

Yet today, throughout the world people continue to suffer and die because they have committed the crime of being born with particular physical characteristics. Everyone is included in this—boys and girls, men and women of all ages. In its classic scenario, the impact of genocide does not limit itself to the victims who are physically exterminated; it also pursues the survivors by denying the suffering they have endured. This revisionism and denial can take many forms.

When a state considers that its population can be classified into unequal genetic categories and uses genetic, and therefore racial, characteristics in the allocation of the rights and duties of its citizens, one must recognize that this is the work of Nazism, be it Hitlerian or tropical. This sort of thinking must be denounced without appeal and stopped before it reaches its logical conclusion, genocide.

But in Rwanda, this absolute evil has already been committed. It has already cost the lives of more than a million people. The hellish images of the exodus from Rwanda imprinted the extermination of these people on the collective conscience of the world. But these images placed the victims and the executioners in the same boat, thereby helping to absolve the killers of guilt.

Today the people of Rwanda are in danger, not in Rwanda itself, but in the camps of Zaire and Tanzania. It is this second Rwanda that, on the strength of falsehoods that are fortunately beginning to be revealed, appears to be a nation in flight from genocide. This is cruel irony when one knows what really happened here.

The population of the refugee camps is being dragged into a sort of collective suicide by the same people who successfully implemented the Rwandan version of the final solution: the administrative and political leadership who are now the privileged partners of humanitarian organizations, the spokesmen of their own hostages, whom some would like to see play a role in this country where they executed more than a million people.

The Missing Population

I would like to talk about the population that has literally disappeared, to talk about the extermination of almost all of the Tutsi racial group that remained in Rwanda despite the cyclical persecution that they have endured since 1959. This ongoing persecution over three decades pushed more than a million Tutsis into exile without a word from the international community. Please note that I do not use what is in my opinion the more derogatory word "ethnicity" that is habitually used to describe the different groups of the Rwandan population.

The social and historical reality of Rwanda is far from this "tri-ethnic" model of Hutu, Tutsi, and Twa. The term "ethnicity" refers to cultural, linguistic, and even sometimes religious traits that everyone in Rwanda shares. I would like to recall (and I do not think that it is a use-less point in view of the way the problems of my country are seen and portrayed abroad) that in Rwanda Hutus, Tutsis, and Twa have shared a common language, customs, beliefs, and history for so long that the origin of this collective memory is lost in time. Similarly, the people who comprise these three categories, which originally represented social rather than ethnic or racial distinctions, were never separated in any lasting way and have always lived together in Rwanda without any kind of "ethnic" grouping.

The Genesis of a Tragedy: Racialization Permitted, then Required

Rwandan society has been artificially "racialized" since the 1920s. Racialization was magnified, sanctioned, and presented as natural law and divine will by various ideologues (mainly foreign missionaries). This racialization was internalized by the "indigenous" elites, who were incapable of foreseeing the tragic consequences of their own alienation. Racialization corrupted the spirit of the emancipation movement of the late 1950s to the point of overtaking it at the time of independence. Then, for close to 35 years, racialization was accepted, glorified, offi-cially implemented on identity cards, sanctioned through racial quotas, and above all justified, through an unbelievable shell game, as the monstrous symbol of democracy.

But who would believe that the foreign supporters of the perpe-trators of the genocide, who justified their support as the supposed democratic will of the majority, could ever imagine a political debate in their own countries based on the hair color of the presiden-tial candidates? It was nonetheless this sort of "genetic" democracy that was accepted as legitimate for more than three decades. Legitimate to the point of justifying genocide, a genocide that today astounds the world! As if after three decades of racist governments, the ideological foundation of the state in Rwanda since the social rev-olution of 1959 could have had any result other than genocide. And today the world asks how to help Rwanda without trying to under-stand this.

Refusal to See the True Face of Tropical Nazism

Why did the international community remain indifferent to the cyclical massacres that resulted in the deaths of tens of thousands of people in 1959, 1961, 1963, 1967, 1973, and on and on? The international community considered them "depressing tribal conflicts" and shrugged their shoulders.

Why wasn't the fundamentally racist and Hitlerian ideology that inspired these massacres denounced? Why did people refuse to see that those who were being killed, and the millions who were being forced into exile, had committed no other crime than being Tutsis? In the eyes of the organizers of these pogroms, physical appearance was presented as the genetic characteristic of a minority race, destined to serve as a ritual sacrifice to democracy and the will of the majority.

And why then, when I sought refuge in Switzerland, was I given *political* asylum? For the *political* activities I was involved in at the age of 12? Of course not! The international community *admitted* in reality the particular position of Rwandan refugees, condemned to perpetual exile on the pretext of "lack of space." They *knew* that for three decades we were more than a million racial refugees, racially persecuted, officially designated as the genetic enemies of our own people by the leaders of the two Rwandan postindependence governments.

Who condemned these leaders for the overt and shameful practice of racial quotas in schools, for their hysterical and obsessive reference to physical traits, those alibis that took the place of a real democratic debate? "Majority Hutus, minority Tutsis"—does one ever hear people say majority Aryan, minority Jew in Europe? Do Europeans ever speak of the brown-haired, dark-eyed majority imposing an absolute quota on the number of ministers with blond hair and blue eyes? Yet this corresponds exactly to differences between Rwanda's "ethnic groups," a reference about which certain humanitarian organizations still inquire in recruiting personnel. How can the international community talk about helping us without trying to understand the source of our problems?

Denial of the Genocide

Today, the international community uses three different methods to deny that the genocide took place in Rwanda.

"TRIBAL" WARFARE

The first is to pass off this conflict as a tribal war between the Hutus and the Tutsis, the result of supposed ancestral hatred that has bloodied our hillsides since the beginning of time. We must remember that before 1959, "racial" war had never occurred in Rwanda. One must also point out that all of the massacres that took place in this country were organized by the state—its police and its soldiers. Rwandan peasants, Hutus or Tutsis, have never spontaneously attacked each other in pseudo-tribal war. To speak of "interethnic conflicts" is therefore a misuse of language.

Suppose that in April, May, and June 1994, a tribal war had taken place in Rwanda. This would mean that everyone was killing everyone else. If everyone is guilty, then in reality no one is. Certainly it was the intention of the planners of the genocide to involve as many people as possible, to implicate everyone in a kind of blood pact. The planners and perpetrators of the genocide intended to present it as yet another manifestation of supposed ancestral hatred that was simply bloodier than the others. This is the first form of denial of our holocaust.

CONFUSION BETWEEN THE GENOCIDE AND
THE EXODUS AND CHOLERA

Another way of confusing the deliberately planned and coldly executed extermination of more than a million of our men, women, children, and aged parents is to argue that the epidemic and the exodus that were the result of the genocide were worse than the genocide itself.

The Rwandan genocide resulted from a deliberate will to exterminate a "racial" group because of what, in the fantasies of the murderers, it represented simply by being born. The epidemics that became the dominant image of the Rwandan drama in the West had no criminal or racist intent. A disease affects everyone it touches without distinction. You will have to pardon these macabre distinctions, but the confusion sometimes found in the international press forces one to make them. Moreover, I must add that the exodus was led and organized by the same people who were responsible for the genocide, as if they were trying to complete their murderous task by killing off the greatest possible number of Rwandans.

THE INTOXICATING FALSEHOOD OF A "SECOND GENOCIDE"

The most recent form of denial of the genocide is to propagate the belief that on the hillsides and in the cities of Rwanda today a second genocide is taking place. It is banalization of the crime and an insult to the innocents who were killed and to humanity itself to present the ongoing insecurity in Rwanda as a second genocide.

President François Mitterand asked, "Do you really believe that the genocide ended with the victory of the Tutsis?" Who in France could resist the easy explanation of "tribal warfare as usual with the blacks?" And above all, who could believe that these blacks, as they are seen in France, would not fall into a countergenocide of their enemies after their total victory?

It is deeply disturbing to realize that a certain part of the Western public has been convinced by the prevailing version of events that can be summarized thus: "The RPF rebels shot down the president's plane, then they began the massacres that led to the exodus of two million people who were helped by France." Do you think that this is a caricature? No, in effect this is what one can find in the most recent version of the *Petit Robert* dictionary.[2]

This same view of a "rebel" movement responsible for the genocide that the government committed against their families and supporters finds expression in the term *"Khmers noir,"* which is still used by the press that continues to support the former government. That certain members of the press regard the RPF and not the *Interahamwe* as resembling the Khmer Rouge reveals the height of cynicism in their coverage of our country's tragedy.

The "Duty of Neutrality" in the Face of a Genocide

According to some people, neutrality is a duty that the international community must impose on itself in order to intervene effectively in a "humanitarian disaster" like that of Rwanda. (It must be noted that it was not a comet that fell on our heads, but the systematic elimination of our families carried out by specific and identifiable actors.)

A neutral attitude implies that they are all the same, that their history is too complicated to understand, that there must be guilt on both sides, and similar theories. Why do some people refuse to identify the killer and the victim of a crime that was committed in broad daylight? In the former Yugoslavia, the international community has clearly identified the Bosnian Serbs as the aggressors. (Which in no way signifies that the action of the international community has been any more effective there.) In the case of Rwanda, the refusal to clearly point out the killers is a crime and an added insult to the victims and the mourning survivors. It is like desecrating mass graves.

One is almost surprised to read the former president of *Médecins Sans Frontières*, Rony Brauman, who in his book about endangered populations makes the amazing observation that "It was the RPF that stopped the genocide, not the international community."[3] Does this then mean that it wasn't *Opération Turquoise*? It is rare to see this expressed in writing or emphasized in any manner by the international media.

The friends who came to help us in our need know that in Rwanda all the actors, active or passive, in this drama will be held in the same disregard. Learn about our history, about the political philosophy that led to this tragedy, but also about the ideas of those who are proposing credible solutions to escape from this infernal cycle, from this racial trap. Learn how to identify the true protagonists. How can Rwandans be reconciled if one does not identify who the opposing parties are, especially since the criminals use this confusion to mask their crimes?

It was the Rwandans themselves who stopped a disgraceful genocide that the whole world, as if in a stupor, was content to watch. These Rwandans had the wisdom to establish a government of national unity. They have controlled the desire for vengeance when, in a situation without precedent in history, the army that ended the genocide belonged to the same group whose supporters were targeted for extermination. The situation the RPF encountered in its defeat of the former Rwandan Armed Forces would be like that of a Jewish army, having defeated the Nazis, coming across the death camps and liberating the survivors.

It is very difficult to imagine the sorrow that these young people faced as they advanced battle after battle, inevitably encountering the bodies of their families and friends, killed simply because they were Tutsis. The memory of the victims of the Rwandan genocide, the unfathomable suffering of the survivors, the restraint of the soldiers who ended the slaughter—all of this should hold a greater place in what we hear about the drama of our country. Stop being suspicious. Sincerely help our government to heal the wounds. Help Rwanda to rise again.

■ FREDERICK GATERA, PROGRAM OFFICER, AUSTRIAN RELIEF PROGRAM

When I hear people in the international community talking about reconciliation between the Tutsis and the Hutus, I think that it is not the Tutsis and the Hutus who need reconciliation. Rwanda needs to reconcile political power and the people. Throughout history, Rwanda has suffered not so much from ethnic conflict as from political conflict.

In 1896 there was a struggle for power in Rucunshu near Gitarama between those who wanted the son of the king to succeed to the throne and those who wanted the son of the queen mother to succeed. In 1932 there was another political conflict when King Musinga was overthrown because he refused to become a Catholic, as ordered by the Belgian colonial administration. In 1959 the Belgians still had control of the country and could have stopped the brewing political crisis and the violence that it created. They didn't. Instead, they stood by as extremist politicians incited Hutu peasants to kill Tutsi peasants.

In December 1963 in the prefecture of Gikongoro, it was not the peasants themselves who spontaneously took up spears and machetes to kill the Tutsis, but rather it was the newly independent government that ordered the massacres. Written testimonies prove it; we know who committed the massacres; we know who organized the massacres. They were arrested and interrogated, and at the end they were all freed. This is what is called impunity. Nowhere have I read that Hutu peasants attacked Tutsi peasants spontaneously on their own initiative. In each incidence it was the government in power that attacked its own population for political reasons. In 1973 the massacres started again, once again for political reasons. It was the legacy of all these massacres that led to the events that began in April 1994.

When the killings started in April, I was in Butare, and I can attest to the fact that the population of Butare had decided not to take part in the massacres. On 19 April, two military planes landed in Butare carrying hundreds and hundreds of soldiers, *paracommandos*.[4] The next day the massacres started in Butare. On 20 April the *paracommandos* began shooting people. They ordered the population to kill all the Tutsis and everyone who belonged to the opposition. Things continued like this until the massive exodus of refugees to Zaire, Tanzania, and Burundi, which everyone will remember from the press coverage.

There have been numerous crises in the history of the country, but if you study them carefully you will see that these crises were not about Hutu peasants killing Tutsi peasants; there were no real differences between Hutu peasants and Tutsi peasants. Each time, these crises were provoked by politicians who used the masses to maintain their power or to take power.

The Second Republic was a bloody dictatorship. President Habyarimana took power in July 1973. Between 1973 and 1977 he murdered the entire ruling class who controlled the country during the First Republic. The ex-president, Gregoire Kayibanda, was killed along with most of his ministers. Everyone who was swept from power was killed. And yet no members of the former regime were Tutsis; they were all Hutus. They were murdered in prison without pity, although they no longer posed a threat, because of the stupidity of the new regime.

Between 1980 and 1986 the dictatorship was consolidated and grew more repressive. Journalists who denounced the tyranny of the regime were usually accused of being insane and a danger to the people. Then they would be thrown in prison and often killed, even if they were Hutus. In 1990, during the War of October, more than 10,000 people were arrested. They were Tutsis, Hutus from the center and south of Rwanda, and members of the opposition. Many of these people died or were killed in prison.

What is astonishing is that, through all of this, no one lifted a finger to condemn the actions of the Habyarimana regime. The Church, which could have condemned these actions as abuses of basic human rights, said nothing. I rarely heard the missionaries condemn these arrests. The international community did not condemn these arrests, but sat back and continued blindly supporting the Habyarimana regime. Even when the arrests were exposed and condemned by human rights groups, they were treated as an African problem. If people who are uncivilized kill or imprison each other then it is too bad, but it can be excused because they are primitive.

In 1991 in the prefecture of Gisenyi, several hundred people were killed in the commune Kibirira. In January 1991 almost the entire

Bagogwe clan were eliminated. In 1992 there were massacres in Bugesera, and bomb attacks began in Kigali, first at the Kigali bus station, then in Ruhango in the prefecture of Gitarama, then in Taba where 30 children were killed by a land mine, etc. And still there was no response. The international community did nothing; no one lifted a finger to stop this repressive dictatorship.

I often ask myself how is it that the international community, which organized a massive intervention to stop Saddam Hussein when he had no intention of massacring large numbers of Kuwaitis but rather wanted to make them part of Iraq, did nothing when the massacres started in Rwanda. It is astonishing how the international community rose up in unison to stop Saddam Hussein, while in Rwanda there were continual massacres and no one moved to stop them. We must all ask ourselves this question.

In May 1993 an important opposition leader, Emmanuel Gapyisi from the MDR,[5] was assassinated. In February 1994 Gatabazi of PSD[6] was assassinated. Gatabazi was a Hutu, not a Tutsi. He was not assassinated because of his ethnic group, but because he opposed the politics and the methods of the Habyarimana regime. Then in April 1994 there was the genocide.

I am still bothered by the use of the word "genocide," because genocide means to attack one ethnic group, while Habyarimana not only attacked the Tutsis, but also attacked Hutus. Habyarimana attacked anyone who appeared to be opposed to the regime, its philosophy or methods. The opposition was considered a major obstacle and had to be eliminated. I ask that each time we use the term "genocide," we try to think seriously about what it means, and be precise. It was not just Tutsis who were killed. Large numbers of Hutus were also massacred. The macabre play put on by the Habyarimana regime opened its first act when a small number of people were systematically eliminated. By the fifth act, in April 1994, it was organizing large-scale massacres.

We can argue back and forth about the definition of the words genocide, ethnicity, and race, but for me all of this is secondary. What is fundamental is to try to understand the mechanisms of this diabolical system that started as a small fire that the world left to burn freely for years, and that in the end became a huge blaze that no one could put out.

■ FAUSTIN KAGAME, JOURNALIST

I have listened to the different speakers here and have asked myself if I am sitting in the right seminar. We have talked about massacres, we have talked about genocide, and we have even said there is a confusion between these two words. I wanted to stress that a genocide is not a massacre. "Genocide" is a specific term. It means killing people for what they are, not what they have done. The Hutu opposition were killed because of their opinions, not because of how they were born.

I want to insist on the fact that genocide has taken place here. Let's not negotiate over the definition of words. There was an intention on the part of certain Rwandans to eliminate an entire, specific group of other Rwandans, not for what they thought, but for who they were. It was for this reason that babies were killed, that old people were killed.

■ DR. MAURICE BUCAGU, DIRECTOR, NATIONAL OFFICE FOR POPULATION (ONAPO)

Can demographic pressure be considered a cause of the genocide in Rwanda? It is not an easy question to answer. Population is tied to politics, so it is not easy to separate the two.

Before beginning my presentation, I want to give you some figures on the population of Rwanda. A census on 15 August 1991 found the population of Rwanda to be 7,149,215 people, with a population density of 271 people per square kilometer and a population growth rate of 3.1 percent. The population of Rwanda will therefore double every 22 years, if the population growth rate remains the same.

I would like to quote a speech that Mrs. Ogata, the United Nations High Commissioner for Refugees, gave at the Cairo Population Summit in September 1994: "The recent strife in Rwanda is a striking example of ethnic conflict, ignited by population pressure and diminishing land resources." This is not a new opinion. I call this the history of Rwanda seen through the distorting prism of Western analysis. All of the Western press came out with this same analysis. They considered Rwanda's genocide to be a case of ethnic hatred and overpopulation— a case of demographic pressure on the meager resources of the country that eventually developed into ethnic hatred.

An objective analysis of what happened in Rwanda since 1990 brings one to the realization that the views of the United Nations High

Commissioner for Refugees are an erroneous interpretation of what is fundamentally a political conflict—a political conflict involving a group of people who took power by force, with the help of Western powers, and who were incapable of managing the affairs of the state in the way the people desired. In the face of growing political opposition, this group used every means to maintain itself in power—in particular, ethnic division.

Can the conflict in Rwanda be linked to secular hatred between Hutus and Tutsis? I would say not. It was exactly 95 years ago that the first order of the French White Fathers arrived in Rwanda. These first Europeans admired the social organization, the strict political hierarchy, the complementary relationship between the activities of the pastoralist and the agriculturalist who shared the same land, the same language, the same culture, and the same calabash of beer or milk.

Historians unanimously agree on these facts. Rwanda and Burundi represent a unique case in Africa, where ethnic groups, even if they were different in the beginning, populated these countries in successive waves of migration and arrived at a perfect symbiosis, giving birth to one people, sharing one language and one culture and living together in peace. Rwanda and Burundi were true nations even before the arrival of the Europeans.

One can look at other examples in Africa such as the different regions of Uganda, where Buganda is inhabited by the Baganda tribe; Toro is inhabited by the Batoro tribe; and Ankole is inhabited by the Banyankole. In West Africa there is Sénégal with Wolof and the Dioula, etc. The concept of different ethnic groups does not apply to the situation in Rwanda. The division between Hutus and Tutsis is in reality a seed that was planted by the colonial powers. Divide and conquer is a well-known method of colonial administration, and one that worked very well in Rwanda. Until the arrival of the European colonialists, no one could give objective criteria for distinguishing Rwanda's so-called ethnic groups. Unfortunately, after independence, the men who held the destiny of Rwanda in their hands used these divisions to maintain power. Since 1959, Rwanda has been ruled by the politics of ethnicity.

One has to question the efficiency and effectiveness of these people who were named to positions of authority without any qualifications in a veritable system of apartheid à la Rwandaise. I am not speaking about this for the first time, as many people have talked about it before, but the international community closed its eyes to this for years.

Now to get back to the problem of population in Rwanda. Did an imbalance really exist between demographic growth and the increase in production? I would say yes. If one looks at figures for 1990, the population growth rate was at 3.1 percent, while the economic growth rate was at minus 2 percent. This imbalance is real, it is a problem, and it is not new. The government should have intervened and found its role in addressing this imbalance. This is what managing the public good is all about.

There are other examples of this imbalance. Land is something to which Rwandans are very attached, yet on average Rwandans have only 0.4 hectares of land per person. Agricultural production in 1992 fulfilled only 70 percent of the daily calorie needs of the population, which meant that there was a caloric production deficit of 30 percent. Health spending covered only 50 percent of the health needs of the population. In education it was the same. There was a lack of quaified personnel in all sectors. All of this contributed to an important disequilibrium between the population and the resources of the country.

But can this imbalance be considered a cause of the crisis in Rwanda? I would say no. If the entire population had been considered as human capital, capable of increasing agricultural production and thereby contributing to the development of Rwanda, then we would not be in this crisis. Instead, the population of Rwanda was used as a weapon to divide the country, a weapon to mobilize killers with the threat of the mortal danger posed by a superhuman race from a foreign country. There was also the promise of redistributing belongings taken from the enemy.

In 1986 there was an official proclamation that said that refugees outside the country no longer had the right to come back to Rwanda. At the most, they would be allowed to briefly visit their families in Rwanda, but only if they promised to leave again. One can say this was the beginning of the genocide. The declaration that the more than two million Rwandans living outside the country could not return was also one of the causes of the war of October 1990. According to the International Declaration of Human Rights, no government can refuse anyone the right to return to his home country. This is yet another example of the poor management of the public good by the government.

If the size of the population was really a problem tied to the genocide, I believe that the organizers of the massacres would have attacked the landowners and the rich, who in reality were the ruling class. But they attacked people who had nothing, people who were excluded from the management of the country by the apartheid system that was in place. We note that it was Rwandans who were suspected, either in reality or potentially, of being opposed to the government or of being members of the political opposition who were eliminated.

The organizers of the genocide were not afraid of population growth or of a lack of economic growth, but of the people who were questioning their management of the affairs of the country. It was the exposure of the corruption, the nepotism, the embezzlement of public funds, and the violations of human rights that the government feared, not population growth. They were incapable of finding solutions and strategies to address the imbalance between natural resources and population. Instead of addressing the real problems of the country, the group in power, which was dominated by extremists who had no interest in or knowledge of democracy, opted for a scorched-earth strategy, for a strategy of massacres and genocide.

■ MAJOR FRANK RUSAGARA, PUBLIC AFFAIRS OFFICER, RWANDAN PATRIOTIC ARMY

Dr. Bucagu has talked about the population, which leads me to question, what is wrong with the Rwandan population? Others have referred to the population as a sponge that absorbs anything. I find this analysis fundamentally wrong. We are all human beings first and foremost, and therefore should be able to judge what is wrong and what is right. To that extent, I cannot apologize for the population of Rwanda for having unleashed terror on their neighbors and their relatives. I cannot apologize for this. Let us talk instead about what makes brothers kill brothers, what makes neighbors kill neighbors. There must be something wrong with the people who do this.

I will venture to trace how all of this came about, and perhaps this will help us in looking forward to a solution. From 1959 to 1994 the population of Rwanda was polarized. A portion of the Rwandan popu-

lation enjoyed government protection and special treatment, while at
the same time another portion of the population was denied their
rights, was being prepared for slaughter. I fled this country in 1961
while I was still in primary school. This was at the height of the independence movement. For my family, the independence movement
meant we were forced to leave Rwanda. The culture of impunity began
with this. There were people who were meant to be protected and people who were meant to die or be chased out of the country.

When genocide or massacres were taking place, even if people did
not directly take part, there was a conspiracy of silence on the part of
the population. In the vocabulary of Rwanda, the regular massacres of
Tutsis were simply called "incidents." But these were planned and organized killings. Yet the academics called them *événements*, mere "incidents." This is a clear case of the Rwandans failing themselves. There
were no demonstrations, there were no protests. Someone at the
University of Butare told me that at the height of the killings there
were professors at the university, professors of medicine, among them
rectors of the university, who were saying to the killers, "We are with
you."

What finally befell the unwitting Rwandan population, intellectuals included? For years the majority of the population of Rwanda was
riding on a tiger's back. When you ride on the tiger's back you may be
strong, but you risk ending up in its mouth. When you talk about the
thoroughness of the genocide, of the huge number of people killed, it
was because of the conspiracy of silence, because of shortsightedness,
and because of something that is fundamentally wrong with Rwandan
society.

I can give you an example of this fissure in Rwandan society. When
the RPA reached Kigali from Kibungo prefecture, someone from
Kibungo, my home commune, came to the house where I was staying.
After so many years as a refugee, I was happy to see someone from my
home commune. We were exchanging our views and experiences
about what had happened to Rwanda. This person, who was the son of
a former minister in the First Republic, had lost his brothers and the
rest of his family. He was recounting the story of how he lost his family, and someone asked, "How could they be killed like that hiding in
their house? Why didn't they run away?" This man said, "But why run
away? Run away from what? They should never have been killed in

the first place." Because he was a Hutu, he and his family thought that they were not supposed to be killed. It was the Tutsis who were supposed to be killed, not the Hutus.

The Rwandan population has a problem. Let's face the facts; let's not absolve the population for what it did. Let us in fact do away with the culture of impunity that created this problem in the first place. Where do we start and how do we address the problem? First, let us take responsibility for what has happened here. Let those who took part in the genocide be punished for it. Let everyone see them punished. Let us see justice done for once. The population of Rwanda participated in genocide, and they must know that this is wrong, that they have no right over the lives and property of other people. They did not respect the lives and property of their neighbors. That's where things went wrong.

Notes

1. With the notable exception of France, which established the *Zone Turquoise*, effectively protecting the organizers of the genocide and allowing them to escape into Zaire.

2. The September 1994 edition of the *Petit Robert* dictionary includes the following summary of the history of Rwanda: "The army intervened in 1973 and General Juvenal Habyarimana took power. He undertook the integration of the Twa minority and his efforts at reconciliation with the Tutsi were opposed by certain groups in the army. In 1990, Tutsi refugees from Uganda, organized as the Rwandan Patriotic Front and joined by various members of the opposition, invaded the country from the north, provoking a limited French intervention and forcing the government to negotiate in 1993. Multi-party democracy was recognized in 1991 (the Arusha Peace Accords). But in April 1994, the RPF assassinated J. Habyarimana on board his plane and launched a major offensive marked by massacres and by the retreat of millions of people to a security zone established by France (*Opération Turquoise*, June 1994) and to Zaire." The newly installed government of Rwanda sued Robert Dictionaries and won, forcing it to rewrite its description of the events in Rwanda.

3. The French humanitarian organization *Médecins Sans Frontières* (MSF), or Doctors Without Borders, has been highly visible in crisis spots around the world, including Rwanda. MSF was active in the

refugee camps in Zaire, but pulled out after vocally denouncing the control that the former government of Rwanda and FAR exerted over the refugees and the flow of humanitarian assistance. Rony Brauman, the former head of MSF, is known for taking strong political stands on humanitarian issues. (See Brauman's "Protection of Civilians in Conflict," in *World in Crisis: The Politics of Survival at the End of the Twentieth Century*, published by *Médecins Sans Frontières* in September 1996.)

4. An elite unit, trained by the French, belonging to the Rwandan armed forces of the former government.

5. *Mouvement Démocratique Républicain*, the Democratic Republican Movement.

6. *Parti Social Démocrate*, the Social Democratic Party.

CHAPTER

THE VOICE
OF EXTREMISM

Introduction

■ **JOHN A. BERRY AND CAROL POTT BERRY**

Members of the former government and their sympathizers were not invited to speak at the seminar for obvious reasons. However, in editing this book, we felt it extremely important to present their perspective and sought out documents that expressed the genocidal philosophy of the former regime in their own words.

The three documents we have chosen are taken from extremist newspapers and radio and from the former govenment in exile in Zaire. Each represents a different phase in the preparation, mobilization, and justification of the genocide. The "Hutu Ten Commandments" and the 3 April 1994 broadcast from RTLM are examples of how Rwandan public opinion was prepared for the genocide. The RTLM broadcast of 5 June 1994 demonstrates how the radio was used to mobilize the genocide by encouraging the population and the army to teach the Tutsis a "final lesson." The longest of the three documents, titled "The

Rwandan People Accuse . . .," is a typical example of self-justifying pro-paganda from the former government. Taken together, these three doc-uments clearly demonstrate the type of premeditated and cynical orga-nization that prepared the people of Rwanda to commit genocide.

"The Rwandan People Accuse . . ." is an open letter addressed to the president of the Human Rights Commission in Geneva and signed by the minister of justice for the government in exile,[1] Agnes Ntamabyaliro. It was printed in Bukavu, Zaire, and dated 21 September 1994. A justification to the world of the former government's role in the genocide, copies of this letter were addressed (in order) to the Pope and to the leaders of the United States, France, Zaire, Tanzania, Uganda, Burundi, the United Kingdom, Belgium, Germany, the United Nations, and the Organization of African Unity.

The distorted logic and paranoid rhetoric of the letter are typical of those used by the architects of the genocide in the former government. The letter argues that the Hutus, who arrived in Rwanda before the Tutsis, have for centuries been the victims of unjust Tutsi oppression, supported by outside powers and imperial interests. These "outside powers" include Uganda, Belgium, the United States, and the United Nations but exclude France (which since 1990 has been the foreign power most heavily involved in Rwanda, albeit in support of its allies in the former government).

The accusations seem even more paranoid when read in detail. They accuse the RPF of crimes against peace, crimes against humanity, and ultimately genocide. The Belgians are accused of complicity in the assas-sination of President Habyarimana, of terrorism, and, ironically, of failing to respond to the obligation to help people in danger. The United States is accused of the same, as well as of conspiring with the RPF and plotting against the Rwandan people under the guise of offering humanitarian assistance. Finally, the United Nations is accused of organizing an unjust arms embargo, failing to respond to the obligation to help people in dan-ger, denial of justice, terrorism, and crimes against humanity.

In the schizophrenic logic of their arguments, the former govern-ment displaces the blame for the genocide, denying its own responsi-bility and instead accusing the RPF and its foreign supporters of orga-nizing a genocide of the Hutus. The accusations against the "outside powers" are even more revealing of the former government's paranoid schizophrenia. The Belgians, Americans, and the United Nations are charged on the one hand of killing President Habyarimana, terrorism, and crimes against humanity and on the other of not offering assistance to the same group that accuses them of these crimes. As editors, we can think of nothing more damning to the former government than to publish a direct translation of its own words.

"The Rwandan People Accuse . . ."

■ **AGNÈS NTAMABYALIRO, MINISTRY OF JUSTICE, REPUBLIC OF RWANDA (BUKAVU, ZAIRE)**

Translated from the French *"Le Peuple Rwandais Accuse . . ."* Bukavu, Zaire: Ministry of Information, 1994.

Introduction

The interethnic conflict that is at the base of the present tragic situation dates back far in time. In effect, anyone who knows the history of Rwanda knows that the country was first inhabited by the Twa (Pygmies) who lived on hunting and gathering. The Hutu (Bantus) farmers came next, and finally, much later, came the Tutsis (Hamites), who occupied themselves exclusively with raising cattle.

Rwanda, divided into Hutu principalities ruled through solid political institutions, was conquered little by little by the Tutsis, who adopted these institutions in their entirety. The Hutus, despite their numerical superiority, were reduced to the rank of serfs. The conflict between the Hutu and the Tutsi had already begun more than four centuries ago.

It is into this context that the colonialists and missionaries arrived. The colonialists even helped the Tutsis to complete their conquest of the entire country. They were in solid support of the power that they found in place.

During this whole time, missionaries were teaching the children of the Tutsi nobility in order to ensure their own succession. But at the same time, a rare few Hutu were also able to benefit from a certain amount of training at their own level.

It was thus much later that these rare Hutu intellectuals proclaimed the rights of the ordinary people which had been monopolized by the feudal nobility (see the "Bahutu Manifesto" of March 1957).

But the king at the time and his entourage reacted brutally to these proclamations, saying that they had nothing in common with reality and that the Hutus had no reason to protest against the Tutsis. This tense situation led inevitably to the Revolution of 1959.

This revolution reestablished liberty and equality between the citizens of Rwanda. Democracy was the basis of power in the Republic that was declared on 28 January 1961, and confirmed by a referendum under the supervision of the United Nations on 25 September 1961.

But those who were opposed to democracy went into exile abroad in order to organize attacks against the young Republic and retake power by force; the last of this series of invasions took place in 1967. From this point on, the enemies of democracy decided on a lull in the fighting to better organize and equip themselves in order to take power by force without difficulty. This is what was attempted on 1 October 1990 by the sons of these refugees known by the name of RPF-*Inkotanyi*.

The Rwandan people have found themselves in a catastrophic situation generally since 1 October 1990, which marks the beginning of the war to reconquer power in Rwanda, and particularly since the ignoble assassination of President Juvenal Habyarimana on 6 April 1994, both being the diabolical work of the RPF-*Inkotanyi*, with the massive support of certain outside powers.

In effect, after so much sweat and blood spilled in the struggle for the defense of national sovereignty, the Rwandan people have, alas, been forced to leave their country and seek exile abroad because on one side the international community decided to break their resistance by declaring a military and arms embargo—one could not have been more unjust!—and on the other side the RPF was daily intensifying their massacres of the Rwandan people.

International opinion was deliberately sheltered from the truth of this situation that was created to serve imperialist interests. Today, the Rwandan people are resolved to reveal to posterity and to history the whole truth of this tragedy and thereby allow men of good will, peace, and justice to do everything that is in their power to help them regain their rights.

This requires proving the responsibility of each one of the principal detractors of the Rwandan people, notably

- The Rwandan Patriotic Front (RPF) or *Inkotanyi*,
- The government of the Republic of Uganda,

- The government of the Kingdom of Belgium,
- The government of the United States of America,
- The United Nations.

I. THE RWANDAN PATRIOTIC FRONT (RPF)–*INKOTANYI*

I.A. *Qualification*

The Rwandan Patriotic Front–*Inkotanyi* is known as a group essentially composed of the descendants of Rwandan refugees in Uganda. They make up a large majority of the Tutsi ethnic group.

During the invasion of Rwanda on 1 October 1990, the military units of the RPF were composed essentially of elements of the National Resistance Army (NRA) of Uganda, under the command of former officers of the same army, among whom one can cite the following:

1. Major General Rwigema, former Vice Minister of Defense of the Government of Uganda who was directing the attack against Rwanda when he was killed on 2 October 1990.
2. Major Kagame, former head of Ugandan Information Services and current Vice President of the RPF and of the Republic (government currently installed in Kigali), Minister of Defense and Chief of Staff of the Army.
3. Major Bayingana, high-ranking officer in the NRA.
4. Major Bunyenyezi, high-ranking officer in the NRA.

Moreover, President Museveni should have declared, as soon as the hostilities by the RPF began, that the invaders of Rwanda were deserters from his army. But this was the same Museveni who was overhead to say at the time, "I know my boys!"

I.B. *Principal Accusations*

In their determination to reconquer power in Rwanda by force, the RPF is guilty of ignominious crimes. In particular, these are crimes against international law, as defined by the statutes of the International Criminal Tribunal of Nuremberg and confirmed by the United Nations in 1945. These crimes are considered as exceptionally grave violations of the rules of international law. Most notably these are the following:

1. Crimes Against Peace

Crimes against peace consist of violations of the rules establishing peace. These are stipulated in Article 6a of the Statute of the International Criminal Tribunal of Nuremberg as "the direction, preparation, setting in motion or pursuit of a war of aggression or of a war violating international treaties, agreements or accords, or the participation in a concrete plan or a plot intended to accomplish one of the above."

Thus, in setting in motion the hostilities by the assassination of the Chief of State, on 6 April 1994, who had taken office in the framework of the Arusha Peace Accords, the RPF deliberately and manifestly violated Article One of those same Accords that stipulates:

> The war between the Government of Rwanda and
> the Rwandan Patriotic Front is over.

It is worth remarking that these events correspond perfectly with the fourth scenario of a preestablished plan by the RPF under the heading "The current and future environment of the organization," which foresees in particular,

- Breaking the Arusha Peace Accords and restructuring of a government, separating by military force Habyarimana and his supporters, in a period not to surpass nine months from the date of the signing of the Peace Accords
- Redefining the transition government
- Organizing elections at a moment judged opportune by the RPF

2. War Crimes

In the terms of Article 6b of the Statutes of the International Criminal Tribunal of Nuremberg, war crimes are "violations of the laws and customs of war." These violations include, without being limited to, "assassination, poor treatment or deportation for forced labor or for any other reason of civilian populations in occupied territories, assassination or poor treatment of prisoners of war, execution of hostages, looting of public or private goods, the destruction without cause of towns and villages or devastation that is not justified for military reasons."

It is worth pointing out that the suppression of war crimes has been laid out in the Hague Conventions of 1907, the Convention on the Prevention and Punishment of the Crime of Genocide or Geneva Conventions of 1949, as well as the Additional Protocols I and II of 1977.

For the RPF, all of these provisions, though sanctioned by international law, were of no importance. Thus, since 1 October 1990 when they began their aggression against the Rwandan people, the RPF has deported a good number of civilians in the territories that it occupies and executed prisoners of war, according to the corroborated testimony of the families of the victims.

Other cases of war crimes can be cited, notably,

* Looting and devastation; for example the equipment of the Mulindi tea factory as well as hundreds of tons of tea that were stocked there[2]
* Massive bombardments, indiscriminate attacks and forced displacement of civilian population

From the beginning of the invasion, the RPF attacked without discrimination—that is they attacked military objectives as well as civilian populations, displacing the latter without respite as combat progressed. These dramatic crimes led to the construction of the sorrowful camps of Miyove, Kisaro, Rutongo, Nyacyonga, etc.

One must remember that some of these camps were the scenes of repeated hostage-taking and bombardments by the RPF that led to the well-known massive exodus of almost the entire Rwandan People.

In the city of Kigali it is sufficient simply to look around to realize how the RPF's massive and indiscriminate bombings damaged civilian infrastructure and buildings.

As for the rest, the representatives of UNAMIR have testified about it more than once:

- Destruction of installations containing dangerous forces: the important electrical generator installations at Ntaruka, the oldest in Rwanda, were the preferred target of the RPF when they were not engaged in other military operations. It is worth remembering that it was over the destruction of this generator that the Minister of Public Works, Felicien Gatabazi, first fell on bad terms with the RPF.

- Attacks on undefended or demilitarized zones: in February 1993, the RPF, in defiance of international law, unscrupulously attacked civilian populations in the demilitarized zones of Byumba and Ruhengeri. It was only after external intervention that the RPF returned to the positions that had been reserved for them.

- Attacks against medical personnel and installations: although international law prescribes the respect and protection of medical personnel and installations, the RPF bombarded the Kigali Hospital Center without a second thought, killing several dozen patients, wounding an equal number, and causing considerable material damage. Neither was the Red Cross Hospital spared, and reports on this matter have been addressed to the authorities concerned. Moreover, the reports of UNAMIR spokesmen have been unequivocal regarding the obvious responsibility of the RPF in this matter.

- Attacks against places of worship: the RPF in its military operations has never demonstrated respect for places of worship. In this respect, we refer notably to the case of the unfortunate individuals who sought refuge in the Sainte Famille Church in Kigali and who were killed during bombardments by the RPF.

3. Crimes Against Humanity

Crimes against humanity constitute violations of the rules of international law, punishable by imprisonment, and consist of acts such as assassination, extermination, slavery, deportation, and any inhuman acts committed against civilian populations before or during a war, as well as persecution for political, racial, or religious motives. To these acts, one must add another specific crime: GENOCIDE.

The heinous crimes committed by the RPF in this period represent crimes against humanity. Thus since the month of November 1990, when the RPF adopted guerilla warfare as a military tactic, numerous deportations and summary executions of civilians were organized in the communes of Muvumba, Kiyombe, Mukarange, Cyumba, and Kivuye in the Byumba prefecture, as well as in the commune of Butare in the Ruhengeri prefecture. Escapees from these regions have willingly testified about them.

The situation that prevailed in these communes later extended to all of the so-called "demilitarized zone," which in reality was under the control of the RPF. Massive and repeated exterminations were in effect documented and denounced.

For example, after the signing of the Arusha Peace Accords on 4 August 1993, acts of assassination and extermination of civilian populations multiplied and intensified.

This was the case with the assassinations in the sub-prefecture of Kirambo (the investigations of these incidents are still in the hands of General Dallaire, former Force Commander of UNAMIR), and in Mutura of Cyohoha-Rukeri and of Remera-Rukoma in the Gitarama Prefecture.

In addition to this, waves of assassinations that occurred throughout the country eliminated members of the Hutu elite, among them: Emmanuel Gapyisi, Fidele Rwambuka, Felicien Gatabazi, Martin Bucyana, etc. It was in the same climate of terror that attacks against, among others, Stanislas Mbonampeka, Donat Murego, and Justin Mugenzi were organized.

It naturally follows that this dramatic situation could only end with the decapitation of the country by the assassination of its president, His Excellency Major General Juvenal Habyarimana, on 6 April 1994.

In effect, President Habyarimana, having already taken the oath of office in the framework of the Arusha Peace Accords, and having on numerous occasions invited the parties concerned to ceremonies installing the institutions of the transitional government, each time came up against the bad faith of the RPF, who were always conspicuous in their unexplained and unjustified absences.

We recall, moreover, that this assassination was part of a macabre plan by the RPF as we have cited above. This assassination was intended to be the detonator of a long string of acts of genocide as we will see below.

4. Genocide

Genocide is a crime against humanity. The International Convention on the Prevention and Punishment of the Crime of Genocide, adopted by the General Assembly of the United Nations on 9 December 1948, states in Article 2:

In the present Convention, genocide is understood to be any one of the following acts, committed in the intention of destroying, in sum or in part, a national, ethnic, social, or religious group, such as

a. Murder of members of the group
b. Grave violations of the physical or moral integrity of members of the group
c. Intentionally submitting the group to conditions of existence that lead to its partial or total physical destruction
d. Measures intended to impede births among members of the group
e. Forced transfer of children of the group to another group

It is appropriate to point out here that from the beginning the RPF took care to categorize in advance the "target groups" of its plan for genocide. This was the "Hutus" in general, especially

• Members of the MRND and CDR political parties
• Those who were qualified as supporters of "Hutu Power" (or Hutu extremists!), that is, Hutus who were members

of the political parties that formerly composed the Committee for Dialogue and who resisted the RPF

Everywhere the RPF troops passed, they systematically killed everyone who they presumed to belong to one of these groups. Thus, as was emphasized by escapees from Byumba Prefecture in their letter to the President of the United Nations Commission on Human Rights dated 24 May 1994, the RPF massacred entire families throughout the region. It is fitting to recall here the essential content of the above-mentioned letter:

> The atrocities redoubled in their intensity after April 1994, especially in the Prefecture of Byumba located in northeast Rwanda. The RPF sowed terror and death in its path to the extent that of the 780,000 inhabitants who formerly comprised the Prefecture of Byumba, only 150,000 people have been located. The majority of them were killed in the most atrocious manner either in displaced persons camps, in the Stadium of Byumba, in the hillsides.

On this subject, here are the poignant testimonies of some of the rare escapees: the Murambi sector (Buyoga commune) that formerly counted 5,155 inhabitants in 1,192 households today registers only 849 displaced persons! The other inhabitants were killed or are missing. In the same way, the RPF killed 50 people who had taken refuge with a person named Nyabirungu and 1,000 people in Rugwangara in the Nyabisiga sector of Buyoga Commune. On 1 May 1994, the RPF killed hundreds of inhabitants of the Cyuru Sector (Kinyami Commune) among whom were found the families of Stanislas Rukanshungirwa (Judge) and Augustin Ubalijoro (Inspector of Education for the sector). The RPF also murdered Abby Mashyenderi of Nyinawimana parish, the priests and nuns of Rwesero Seminary, and all of the inhabitants of Nyamiyaga Sector (Kinyami).

At the same time, the Belgian newspaper *Le Soir*, in its edition of 18 May 1994, published accusations of massacres committed by the RPF against the civilian Hutu population in the Kibungo Prefecture in southeast Rwanda (at the Rwanda-Tanzania border) where "at least 2,000 people have been killed in six weeks." According to this paper, "the UNHCR witnessed deliberate firing upon refugees fleeing Rwanda, villagers assembled in school buildings and cut to pieces with machetes and people thrown alive with their hands and feet tied into the Akagera river." They continue saying that "according to the testimony of refugees, the situation remains very violent in southeast Rwanda." At the border with Tanzania, a representative of the UNHCR saw soldiers of the RPF firing at refugees crossing the river to reach Tanzania, declared the spokesman for the United Nations High Commissioner for Refugees, Rupert Colville. Refugees coming from several dozen villages reported that RPF soldiers killed and tortured Rwandans before throwing them in the Akagera river.

These facts were confirmed by the Government of Uganda itself, which, on 22 May 1994, declared as a disaster zone the districts bordering on Lake Victoria because the water of the lake was contaminated by the bodies carried down the Akagera river, its principal tributary.

At the same time, people from the Kigali and Kibungo Prefectures provided further details and confirmed this information in the following letter addressed to the President of the United Nations Security Council dated 24 May 1994:

> In effect, the zones controlled by the RPF have become zones of death. We, representing the escapees from the Kigali and Kibungo Prefectures and from the camp of Gitarama, are profoundly saddened to bring the atrocities, to which we are eyewitnesses, to the attention of the Institution which you lead. A few concrete examples, chosen from so many others, will give you an idea of the

barbarity of this "Front" that pretends to bring democracy to the Rwandan People.

Kigali Prefecture, Gikoro Commune, Gicaca Sector [near the paved road between Kigali and Rusumo]:

- Thursday, 21 April 1994: close to 3,000 people were machine-gunned to death. The same scene was repeated near the Communal Office at Musha in the Gikoro Commune where the dead bodies were thrown into the shafts of a mine of the former SOMIRWA (Mines Company of Rwanda).

Bicumbi Commune (bridge between Bicumbi Commune and the Bugesera region):

- More than 4,000 people were massacred and their bodies thrown in the Akagera River.

Kibungo Prefecture, Rutonde Commune, Kigabiro Sector:

- The entire Twa population was massacred (the Twa are the least numerous ethnic group after the Tutsis).

Nsinda Sector:

- All of the Hutu population of the Nsinda sector (Rutonde) and Kabare (Muhazi) were assembled next to a mosque near the paved road from Kigali to Rusumo and machine-gunned to death.

Mugesera Commune:

- Hundreds of people were massacred at the Zaza school. Moreover, the entire population of the sectors bordering on Lake Mugesera (Gatare, Nyange, Kagashi, Matongo, etc.) were surrounded and shot or forced to drown.

Rusumo Commune:

- Close to 250,000 displaced people from the communes of Byumba and Kibungo were stopped not far from the Rwanda-Tanzania border. The

international media spoke about them. The RPF
massacred more than half of them; the bodies
were thrown into the Akagera River.

In addition to these massive massacres, other
inhuman practices were used by the RPF. For
example, scenes of cannibalism have been organized;
people are forced to eat human flesh before being
physically eliminated in their turn. People are strung
up alive, others are abandoned with their eyes
gouged out. Pregnant women are disembowelled
and members of the family are forced to eat the fetus
before being eliminated.

The elimination of the Hutu elite affected all the socio-
professional categories of Rwanda, to the point of assassi-
nating men of the church. Thus, at Kabgaye, the RPF on
8 June 1994 assassinated three Catholic bishops, Monsignor Vincent Nsengiyumva, Archbishop of Kigali;
Monsignor Thaddee Nsengiumva, Bishop of Kabgaye; and
Monsignor Joseph Ruzindana, Bishop of Byumba (all of
Hutu ethnicity), as well as dozens of other priests and hundreds of other people who had taken refuge since the
resumption of hostilities.

These acts, with the military victory of the RPF, ended
up spreading through the entire country and continue to
sow desolation among the population that did not have the
chance to escape from Rwanda in time.

In this regard, the results of a survey organized by
Allison Des Forges, a representative of Human Rights
Watch—Africa, as well as the testimony gathered by
the Dutch nongovernmental organization NOVIB, are
conclusive.

• In the first place, the RPF committed intense massacres.
  Hundreds of people were gathered together and massa-
  cred in the Mukingi Commune (Gitarama), in the city of
  Butare and in the Kigali Prefecture. The proof is there.

- NOVIB maintains to have proof that the RPF killed numbers of people in Virunga Park on 3 and 4 August 1994.

Besides which, the media have recently revealed mass graves containing thousands of bodies that have been discovered throughout the country and the RPF has refused to allow the UNAMIR II[3] to visit these sites.

Finally, the Ministry of Justice of the government installed in Kigali has itself recently admitted that soldiers of the RPF have killed Hutus "for reasons of vengeance."

One cannot forget that the RPF was conceived and created to kill! Its soldiers have done nothing but kill! And today they still do nothing but kill!

II. THE REPUBLIC OF UGANDA

II.A. *Qualification*

It is fitting to remember from the beginning that it was the Republic of Uganda that trained the soldiers of the RPF who, for the most part, were full-fledged members of the Ugandan Army (NRA).

On the other hand, the territory of Uganda served as a permanent training ground and base (sanctuary) for the RPF. In short, the Republic of Rwanda was, in a certain manner, attacked by the Republic of Uganda as will be shown in the following charges:

II.B. *Principal Accusations*

1. Uganda Has Attacked Rwanda

As stated above, it was members of the Ugandan Army who, with material and logistical means provided by the same Army, began the war against Rwanda. As proof:

a. As was mentioned above, must we recall that it was President Museveni who declared publicly at the beginning of the war that the RPF were "deserters from his army." And later he said, "I know my men well. . . ." It must be emphasized that "his men" were among the highest ranking officers of the Ugandan Army:

- Major General Rwigema, ex-Vice Minister of Defense in Uganda
- Major Kagame, former Chief of Ugandan Information Services
- Major Bayingana, high-ranking officer in the NRA
- Major Bunyenyezi, high-ranking officer in the NRA

b. When the RPF violated the ceasefire of 8 February 1993, a Mercedes-Benz truck registered in Uganda (UWT 868) was captured by Rwandans of the Ruhengeri military sector. The order placing the truck at the disposition of the RPF was signed by Lieutenant Colonel Benon Tumukunde, Commander of the Ugandan Military Police.

c. Messages from the RPF intercepted after 7 April 1994, date of the resumption of hostilities, prove that Uganda was fighting on the side of the RPF. This concerns notably the following messages:

c.1. Intercepted message 15A755B April 94 from Mbarara for Gatuna. "The NRA is with us and the morale of our troops is high. Re-supply by plane is very efficient and should be continued . . . camouflage your positions and the presence of mercenaries as well . . . remain in contact with the advance elements who will put us in permanent contact with our agents in the capital."

c.2. Intercepted message 141010B April 94. From Kabarore for Ibanda. "We are expecting to hold the NRA in reserve as long as the Belgians are capable of providing us with enough troops to support us against Rwanda (who is being supported by Zaire and France). The buses from the NRA have already arrived while, everyone knows, particularly the Ugandans, that the financial means, material, and logistical support from the Ugandan Army risk being slow in coming. Especially with the participation of foreigners who are supporting us militarily, it seems that the Armed Forces of Rwanda are in no hurry to push out the RPF."

c.3. Intercepted message 040745B May 1994. From Rubindi for Kabarore. "For several weeks the war has been particularly focused on the ethnic front. Uganda is another front about which we have spoken. It is estimated that present good relations between the RPF and Museveni will play an active role. These could allow for discreet mediation to improve relations between us. On this point the message of the Government is unambiguous." Telegram number INT/OPS/94/995 of 041616B from Commander OPS Gisenyi.

c.4. Intercepted message 041130B May 94. From Mbarara for Kiosoro-Kamwezi-Gatuna-Kasese. "In the country of the Leader, the socioeconomic and political situation improves more and more. The Leader supports us 100% and 10,000 men are officially available for us. In addition, all the troops of the NRA in your ranks are also with you.

"Ground and air transportation are provided through the Leader's channels. Re-supply and the evacuation of the seriously wounded will continue to take place without difficulty. Instructors are available for all of your sectors. The movements of white mercenaries must continue to be covered up by elements of the NRA.

"The death squads continue with the massive extermination of the 02 population in the framework of ethnic cleansing. The new regime in power, exclusively composed of MRND-CDR, organizes and leads exterminations without shame. . . . In Gatuna, Kamwezi, and Biri (Kib) our troops control the situation after having saved a few rare survivors of the 02 population pursued by the RPF. All of our accomplices in the zone have been killed. This is the payback of assassins.

"In the south of the country, our troops continue with preparations as planned and are awaiting instructions. We must organize ourselves to fight against PALIPEHUTU-CDR in our sub-region."

After the news of the assassination of President Habyarimana, the attitude of the President of Uganda, Yoweri Museveni, was unequivocal. His intentions were revealed in the May 1994 issue (number 272) of the review *Africa International*. The magazine states:

> From the day after the crash, Yoweri Museveni continued to attend the Pan-African Congress, without changing his schedule in the slightest. In introducing his speech on the role of science in development, in front of an audience still shocked by the news, he discussed the deaths of the two presidents in a particularly detached tone. "It's dramatic, but I have always said that Africans must resolve their own conflicts, otherwise outsiders get involved in them."

And the magazine continued:

> Strange statement. How can one already begin to talk about foreign intervention, or in any case, non-Rwandan intervention in this affair?

Later, the magazine states:

> Museveni, in a joking tone, questioned the cause of such an "accident." "A bomb on board, or fire from the ground?" The whole thing ended with a joke about security services. The hall began to laugh. . . . It is obvious, the President of Uganda made no effort to appear affected by the disappearance of two of his colleagues who he was seen to embrace the day before. . . . In front of the entire assembly of Pan-Africanists, Museveni did not even ask to observe a minute of silence. In a conversation on Sunday 10 April 1994, the Ugandan Chief of State explained at length how the claims of the exiled Tutsis were well founded and reproached Habyarimana for not,

on his own initiative, having sought dialogue with them, despite his multiple recommendations to do so. Then he concluded, "You know it was time to solve the matter."

III. THE GOVERNMENT OF THE KINGDOM OF BELGIUM

III.A. *Qualifications*

Former Trustee of Rwanda, Belgium demonstrated a positive attitude in the Rwandan Revolution of 1959 that ended the feudal monarchy and proclaimed national independence.

Today, the group in power ignores the history of Belgian/ Rwandan relations and supports the restoration in Rwanda of a Tutsi state, one that the people have so firmly denounced.

III.B. *Principal Accusations*

1. Responsibility in the Assassination of the President of the Republic, His Excellency Major General Juvenal Habyarimana.

   Belgium must shoulder a large part of the responsibility for the assassination of President Juvenal Habyarimana. In effect, it was the Belgian contingent of UNAMIR that was in charge of the security of the city of Kigali and especially that of the Gregoire Kayibanda International Airport at Kanombé. It is obvious that in these conditions the Belgian contingent could not have ignored the minute preparations required to commit such a crime.

   As a consequence, the Belgian authorities were, or should have been, informed of the existence of such a macabre plot; they apparently did nothing to prevent the execution of this plan.

2. Complicity in the Attack on Kigali by the RPF.

   The Belgian contingent of UNAMIR contributed greatly to the preparations for the retaking of Kigali by the RPF.

   Thus, under the pretext of convoying supply teams to the unit stationed at the CND in Kigali, the Belgian contingent of UNAMIR helped the RPF to build depots for arms and munitions and helped RPF soldiers to infiltrate the city and the surrounding area.

One must remember that the Belgian contingent always refused to allow inspection of its trucks, which were always covered, despite multiple suspicions and objections at the time.

Besides, was it not discovered later that during the height of the combat the positions of the RPF coincided exactly with those of the Belgian elements of UNAMIR (residences, the Hotel Meridien, Hotel Rebero l'Horizon, King Fayçal Hospital, etc.)?

As well, the testimony of people who were trapped at Amohoro Stadium when the hostilities began indicate that materiel (tanks, armored vehicles, etc.) from the Belgian contingent of UNAMIR were consistently used in looting several places in Kigali.

This was confirmed elsewhere by *Africa International* in its May 1994 issue (number 272, page 7) where it states:

> After the murder of the President . . . eyewitnesses in
> Kigali confirmed that the RPF fought the Presidential
> Guard with equipment furnished by Belgian troops.

3. Terrorism

The Belgian element of UNAMIR was married to the RPF in act and in cause to such a point that between them they maintained a climate of terror for anyone who did not share the ideas of the RPF. As an illustration, one can cite, among others, the nighttime attack against the residence of Jean Bosco Barayagwiza, one of the great leaders of the CDR, at the beginning of this year.

One will recall that the assailants were supposed to be repatriated to Belgium for this reason . . . but no one knows more!

4. Lack of Respect for the Obligation to Help People in Danger

At the same time that Rwanda was put to a rude test by an unjust war started by an overly equipped enemy who crushed everything in their path and kept an entire people at bay and forced Rwanda to resort to a legitimate defense by all means, the Government of Belgium, instead of intervening to avoid the worst, contented itself with recalling its contingent from UNAMIR and saving only its own citizens.

It is to be noted that an important part of UNAMIR's military equipment came from Belgium and as a consequence, the retreat of the Belgian troops signified nothing more than depriving UNAMIR of its capacity to intervene in the Rwandan conflict.

IV. THE GOVERNMENT OF THE UNITED STATES OF AMERICA

IV.A. *Qualification*

The United States of America constitutes, without contest since the fall of the Soviet bloc, the greatest power in the world in all respects. In the framework of NATO and other organizations where they share interests, the United States is an important ally of Belgium. The United States, who is a privileged partner of the United Kingdom, shares the same relationship with Uganda, who is their protégé.

The leadership of the RPF were trained in the United States in Kansas, Louisiana, New Mexico, California, and Oregon. Among the officers of the RPF who benefited from this training is Paul Kagame, head of the Army of the RPF.

In this regard, the magazine *Africa International*, in its edition of May 1994 (number 272) reports that in 1990, the President of the Ugandan Democratic Coalition, Remigius Kinut, had an interview with an official at the Pentagon in charge of the training of Ugandan soldiers in the United States, Tom D. Marley, and was informed that seven of the so-called "Ugandan soldiers" who were trained in the United States were RPF guerrillas.

It was definitely the combination of all of these interests and affinities that justified the intervention of the United States on the side of the RPF in the Rwandan conflict. And it is not to be forgotten that the tendency of the Anglophone world is to spread their influence in Francophone countries.

IV.B. Principal Accusations

1. Complicity with the RPF

At the same time that the Rwandan people were waiting for the implementation of the Arusha Peace Accords, the RPF, for its part, reopened hostilities against Rwanda.

Instead of intervening in one way or another in order to avoid the worst, the American Administration conceived and developed a plan, which was presented to the Security Council, to break the resistance of the Rwandan people through an arms embargo in order to facilitate the victory of the RPF. This led to the adoption, by the Security Council, of Resolution 918 of 17 May 1994.

2. Lack of Respect for the Obligation to Help People in Danger

From the beginning of the hostilities against the Rwandan people by the RPF, the American Administration did nothing to prevent the carnage that was nonetheless foreseeable. They contented themselves in repatriating their citizens, leaving the Rwandan people to be slaughtered.

3. Plotting under Operation "Support Hope"

At the time when, thanks to the embargo declared by the United Nations Security Council, the RPF was conquering an empty country, the surviving population being forced to flee into exile, the American Administration thought up an operation capable of bringing the Rwandan people back under the yoke of the RPF.

In effect, Operation "Support Hope" was conceived in order to reduce direct aid to refugees and to entice the population in exile by concentrating all food aid inside the country they abandoned. This Machiavellian maneuver was too heavy-handed to escape the vigilance of the population, even though they were starving.

V. THE UNITED NATIONS

V.A. *Qualification*

The United Nations is an organization of universal vocation. Since the breakup of the Soviet Union, this organization has become a monolithic machine under the considerable influence of the West in general and the United States of America in particular. This is to say that, in principle, the United Nations adopts any project or resolution that is proposed by this great power.

V.B. *Principal Accusations*

1. Unjust Embargo Against the Rwandan People

Resolution 918 of the United Nations Security Council decreed an embargo against Rwanda that was unjust in more than name.

  a. The embargo struck only the victim, that is to say Rwanda, while the aggressor was not at all bothered.
  b. The embargo did not take into account the fact that it was a declared war.

In effect, the war that was forced upon Rwanda was always categorized as a civil war; that is, a war between two Rwandan parties. Yet the embargo declared by the United Nations affected only one party. The embargo had no other effect than to prevent the Rwandan people from exercising their legitimate right to self-defense, and to reinforce, in a very obvious way, the RPF and therefore prove yet again that this cursed war was not a civil war, but an open war between Rwanda and Uganda.

2. Complicity in Crimes Against Humanity

The attitudes and actions of the United Nations in the Rwandan conflict were of the sort that eased the work of the RPF in violating the Arusha Peace Accords, which for the Rwandan People were the sole pillar of a durable peace.

In effect, it was the responsibility of the international community, which initiated and went along with the negotiation process of the Arusha Peace Accords, to undertake every useful measure to ensure its implementation.

Nonetheless, in the face of the grave threats by the RPF against Jacques Roger Booh-Booh, Special Representative of the United Nations Secretary General, who spared no effort to bring the two parties to a compromise, the United Nations did nothing more than to maintain a low profile—to the point of driving Jacques Roger Booh-Booh to pull out, leaving the field open for General Dallaire, the unconditional ally of the RPF, in violation of the Arusha Peace Accords.

3. Denial of Justice and Lack of Responsibility

The United Nations Assistance Mission to Rwanda (UNAMIR) had, among other missions, that of assuring the security of the so-called "demilitarized" zone and the city of Kigali. Before the end of 1993, assassinations that easily count as "genocide" were committed by the RPF, in particular in the Kirambo Subprefecture and at Cyohoha-Rukeri. To date, no investigation of these crimes has ever been undertaken.

In the same way, no known investigations have been undertaken concerning the cowardly assassination of President Habyarimana committed at the International Airport at Kanombé, in UNAMIR's zone of control.

4. Complicity in the Attack Against the City of Kigali

As the Belgian contingent of UNAMIR, which was in charge of security for the city of Kigali, was under United Nations command. See what was said on this subject above.

5. Terrorism

Following the acts of terrorism committed by a unit of UNAMIR in charge of security in the city of Kigali, notably the nighttime attack on the residence of Jean Bosco Barayagwiza, no reaction on the part of the UNAMIR commander has been given to this day.

6. Lack of Respect for the Obligation to Help People in Danger

At the same time that Rwanda became the object of aggression of the RPF in April 1994, the International Community was guilty of adopting a wait-and-see attitude. In effect, nothing was done to prevent the decline of a situation while all indications were that it would indeed worsen. For these reasons, the Rwandan people call on the international community, as well as all people of good faith, to do all in their power to

• Reestablish the truth by every means at their disposition, keeping in mind that a social and historical investigation must precede any legal investigation.

- Reestablish the rights of the Rwandan People, notably by

    a. Giving them serious and real guarantees in order to return to Rwanda
    b. Rehabilitating the Arusha Peace Accords as the only acceptable compromise between Rwandans for a durable peace based on a true democracy
    c. Envisioning all possibilities to render equitable justice to punish the truly guilty and to rehabilitate the innocent

Editor's Notes

[These notes do not represent the viewpoint of the editors of *Genocide in Rwanda: A Collective Memory*, but that of the editors of the Ministry of Information of the Interim Government of Rwanda who originally released *"Le Peuple Rwandais Accuse . . ."* in French.]

1. From the facts presented in this document, it is clear that the RPF unquestionably bears primary responsibility for the war that, since October 1990, has cast a gloom over the Rwandan people and plunged them into indescribable misery.

    - The RPF took the initiative in starting the war against a country that had known peace and political stability for more than 20 years and that many African and European observers held up as a model.
    - The RPF displaced from their lands more than five million peasants, welcoming them to live in poverty on the pretext that Tutsi refugees had known 30 years of exile, as if Rwanda should be a land of competing horrors.
    - The RPF resuscitated the ancient demon of ethnicity by systematically massacring Hutu leaders, elite and people everywhere on their path.
    - Throughout the peace negotiations and the discussions for the installation of the broad-based government and parliament, the RPF fomented factionalism by excluding certain individuals, who hardly qualified as Hutu extremists, with the goal of establishing the dominance of the Tutsi minority.

- Even after the signature of the Arusha Peace Accords, the RPF refused to behave like a normal political party, preferring to be a political-military organization and aiming to take power by the force of arms. The RPF never wanted to end the hostilities and to sit down at the negotiating table, despite the positive disposition of the Government of Rwanda and the recommendations of the international community.
- The RPF planned and executed the assassination of the president of the Rwandan Republic, thus provoking the wrath of the Rwandan people.

2. The other parties responsible for the sad events that have left Rwanda in mourning are all those who allowed themselves to be manipulated and abused by the propaganda of the RPF and its African and European supporters and who were used to transmit the same.

- The heads of the Western media must examine their consciences and judge the harmful influence that some of their journalists played in this war. In effect, the lack of rigor and objectivity that characterized the news on Rwanda is shameful for a press that pretends to support democracy and human rights.

3. In this tragic situation, we cannot be silent about the responsibility of certain international donors who financed these so-called human rights organizations and phoney local NGOs that, in effect, served merely as screens for the political-military activities of the RPF. In the belief that they were financing the democratization of the country, they were, in fact, financing the war of the RPF.

- By simply copying Western plans for democratization onto a complex African reality, certain international donors and certain NGOs favored and helped those who slyly presented themselves as the representatives of the weak and the oppressed or the so-called social change actors, but who in reality were nothing more than the representatives of a minuscule group thirsty for power, and using, in order to gain their ends, the most anti-democratic means possible: war.

- The political history of Man has already shown that a minority that takes power by force, even with the support of an outside power, cannot govern without continually resorting to violence. The supporters of the RPF and those who have adopted a policy of complacency toward the Front should remember this.
- Unless the vague hegemonic desires of the RPF and President Museveni can be discouraged, Rwanda and the African Great Lakes Region will continue to know war and political instability for a long time.
- The international community (governments, NGOs, etc.) and all people who value peace and liberty must rouse themselves from their lethargy to help Rwandans to put an end to this war and to rediscover the path to peace and development.

4. The end of hostilities, the resumption of negotiations, the re-establishment of mutual confidence, the rejection of the use of force to gain power and the organization of free and democratic elections remain the only hope for a return to peace in Rwanda and in the region.

The Hutu Ten Commandments
JOHN A. BERRY AND CAROL POTT BERRY

Introduction
The "Hutu Ten Commandments" was published in *Kangura*, a crudely racist newspaper distributed on the streets of Kigali, in December 1990. It is a typical example of the kind of material published by the extremist press in the wake of the 1990 invasion and the 1993 signing of the Arusha Peace Accords. During this period a number of extremist publications vilifying the Tutsis were printed in Kinyarwanda and sold by street vendors. They were largely ignored by the international community at the time of their printing.

In preparing popular opinion for the genocide, the "Hutu Ten Commandments" attacks Tutsi women, describes association with Tutsis as treason, and calls on Hutus to "stop having mercy" on the Tutsis. The influence of this type of hate propaganda was seen during the genocide when Tutsi women were a particular target for rape, sexual slavery, brutal disfigurement, and murder. During the genocide, the treason of opposing Hutu extremist ideology or of having mercy on the Tutsis was often punishable by death. Hutus who attempted to protect Tutsis were forced either to kill them or to be killed themselves. Although racist publications like *Kangura* were often indirect in the call for action against the Tutsis, the climate of racial hatred they fomented prepared Hutus for the genocide.

"Hutu Ten Commandments"

1. Every Muhutu[4] should know that a Mututsi woman, wherever she is, works for the interest of her Tutsi ethnic group. As a result, we shall consider a traitor any Muhutu who

   - Marries a Tutsi woman
   - Befriends a Tutsi woman
   - Employs a Tutsi woman as a secretary or a concubine

2. Every Muhutu should know that our Hutu daughters are more suitable and conscientious in their role as woman, wife and mother of the family. Are they not beautiful, good secretaries and more honest?

3. Bahutu women, be vigilant and try to bring your husbands, brothers and sons back to reason.

4. Every Muhutu should know that every Mututsi is dishonest in business. His only aim is the supremacy of his ethnic group. As a result, any Muhutu who does the following is a traitor:

   - Makes a partnership with Batutsi in business
   - Invests his money or the government's money in a Tutsi enterprise
   - Lends or borrows money from a Mututsi
   - Gives favours to Batutsi in business (obtaining import licenses, bank loans, construction sites, public markets, etc.)

5. All strategic positions, political, administrative, economic, military, and security should be entrusted only to Bahutu.

6. The education sector (school pupils, students, teachers) must be majority Hutu.

7. The Rwandan Armed Forces should be exclusively Hutu. The experience of the October 1990 war has taught us a lesson. No member of the military shall marry a Tutsi.
8. The Bahutu should stop having mercy on the Batutsi.
9. The Bahutu, wherever they are, must have unity and solidarity and be concerned with the fate of their Hutu brothers.

   • The Bahutu inside and outside Rwanda must constantly look for friends and allies for the Hutu cause, starting with their Bantu brothers.
   • They must constantly counteract Tutsi propaganda.
   • The Bahutu must be firm and vigilant against their common Tutsi enemy.

10. The Social Revolution of 1959, the Referendum of 1961, and the Hutu Ideology, must be taught to every Muhutu at every level. Every Hutu must spread this ideology widely. Any Muhutu who persecutes his brother Muhutu for having read, spread, and taught this ideology is a traitor.

Hate Radio: Incitement to Genocide

■ JOHN A. BERRY AND CAROL POTT BERRY

Introduction

The following examples of the use of radio as an incitement to genocide are translations taken directly from *Radio-Télévision Libre des Mille Collines* (RTLM) broadcasts, the first made just before the beginning of the genocide and the second made a month after the killing had begun. The first broadcast, made three days before the president's plane was shot down, offers a haunting premonition of what was to come, referring to specific dates for a "final attack," exhorting people to "stand up" and support the army, and even making oblique reference to the demise of Habyarimana.

The second broadcast was based upon a letter written to RTLM by the management of the Saint Fidele Higher School for Management and Training in Gisenyi. This letter was dated 23 May 1994 and read by Georges Ruggio, a Belgian journalist working for RTLM. This letter was read immediately after a news broadcast and is in many ways typical of the information broadcast on RTLM. News, opinions, and unsubstantiated rumors were interspersed within the same broadcast, creating intentional confusion among listeners, who often relied on RTLM as their sole source of information about the outside world. Letters such as this one from RTLM listeners were read frequently over the air, some making thinly veiled threats and others calling for more direct action.

Ruggio was in a unique position as a foreign journalist working directly for the radio station that became the voice of the genocide in Rwanda. Ruggio, a Belgian citizen, first came in contact with Hutu extremists in Brussels. Through his association with François Nahimana and his circle, Ruggio was invited to Kigali and began making French-language broadcasts on RTLM. Ruggio continued to broadcast on RTLM throughout the war and participated actively in the call to genocide. He fled to Zaire with retreating government forces, continuing to broadcast from RTLM's mobile radio unit.

Although RTLM is now well known as the "killer radio," it began as a private radio station sanctioned by the government of Rwanda and justified by the rhetoric of a free and independent press. The "television" in RTLM's name never really materialized, but the radio station that did operate was neither free nor independent, and completely ignored the principles of fair and responsible journalism. (Before the genocide, the "free" in RTLM's name was jokingly perceived as a reference to its free interpretation of the truth.)

After soliciting investment from private Rwandans, RTLM began broadcasting on 8 July 1993 with a combined format of music, news, editorials, talk shows, and letter reading. During the genocide, RTLM was used to mobilize the population to kill Tutsis through its news and editorial broadcasts (including the now famous call to "fill up" the half-empty graves with Tutsis). RTLM also issued specific instructions to the population about where Tutsis were suspected of hiding, exhorting the killers to "do their duty."

In Rwanda, as in most of Africa, radio remains the most effective means for reaching the masses. Radio ownership among both urban and rural populations in Rwanda is relatively high, and there is a noted tendency among illiterate peasants to believe that anything said on the radio is the truth. RTLM exploited these facts to the maximum in preparing and orchestrating the genocide.

Because RTLM broadcast in Kinyarwanda, the international community in Rwanda largely ignored its racist and provocative broadcasts before the genocide. Even after the genocide began and RTLM's role in provoking violence became clear, the international community refused to jam its broadcasts. After the fall of Kigali, RTLM broadcast from mobile transmitters in Zaire, which could have been located and jammed by American or European military units in the region.

Broadcasts from Radio-Télévision Libre des Mille Collines (RTLM)

RTLM Broadcast, 3 April 1994
(Translated from Kinyarwanda by Faustin Kagame)

Note from the Translator

This recording of RTLM was made on Easter Sunday, 3 April 1994. The original presentation was in Kinyarwanda and was later translated into French. The recording was made on a small Sony "Flat Mic" cassette recorder. RTLM broadcast on FM radio and was, at times, very clear. I was reporting from the CND, the former parliament building of the single-party government, where 600 RPF troops were bivouacked as part of the Arusha Peace Accords of 4 August 1993.

In this translation, the RTLM announcer confirms twice that on 3, 4, and 5 April, or on 7 and 8 April, a "small thing" will happen. The date of 6 April is skipped the first time. The second time, the speaker specifies that "they [the RPF troops] are going to rest" on this date, before continuing the "small thing" on 7 and 8 April. It was on 6 April in the evening that the plane carrying President Habyarimana was shot down, signaling the start of the war and of the genocide.

"And now, the Tutsis, these who have eaten lion,[5] who have eaten lion and who are with the RPF, they want to take power. To take it by force of arms. They want to do a 'small thing,' they want to do this small thing during the Easter holidays, and they even say that they have dates. They have dates, and we know them.

"In fact, they would do better to calm down. We have agents, yeah, heh, ha! [Voice rises until it breaks.] Our agents are there with the RPF, we have agents who send us information. They tell us the following: On 3, 4, and 5 April they say that there will be a small thing, here in Kigali, Kigali City. From today [3 April], Easter, tomorrow, and the day after tomorrow, a small thing is planned for Kigali City. And even on the 7 and 8 April. And then you will hear the sound of many bullets, you will hear grenades exploding.

"I hope that the Rwandan armed forces are on guard. There are the *Inziabwoba* [the fearless ones] who have many, many armed troops, I cannot count them all. The *Inkotanyi* [the 'fierce fighters'—RPF] who have run into them, it is they who know them. They are the ones who know them better than I. Because they, they have run into them and they know the way that they were treated. Or those who attacked Nyamagumba [fortified hill near Ruhengeri; i.e., attackers were RPF], it is they who can tell us how the vultures found something to eat.

"But otherwise, to hold Kigali, we know how to do it, we know how to do it. On 3, 4, and 5 April, we expect this small thing will happen here in Kigali, and then they will follow up and rest on the date of the 6 April, and on 7 and 8 April they are going to do another small thing, using their bullets and their grenades. But in reality, there will be the attack *Simusiga* ['save no more,' i.e., the final attack] that they are waiting for and expecting. And they say, 'When we have finished with this small thing to stir up the town, we will then throw ourselves into the *Simusiga* attack.' But as for the date, my agent [in the RPF] has not yet told me, he has not yet told me.

"There are, nonetheless, Tutsis who are humble, who come to Noheli [the announcer] and who say, 'We want democracy,' and they even gave me this information. And so what? Isn't it like this that it really happens? What can we do? What can we do? Tutsis who really are humble, they are asking, be it by radio, be it in the newspapers, they are proclaiming from the bottom of their hearts as they say in Kinyarundi [the language of Burundi], they are saying to the RPF, 'These things that you want to do over the course of the Easter holidays, they don't have the least bit of interest for the Rwandan people.' The humble Tutsis, they say, 'These things, these disturbances, this bloodletting, we have had enough of them. You [the RPF] should know the Rwandan military, the armed forces of this country, you are going to put them [these soldiers] at our backs, yet this is not necessary. This is going to provoke them, the armed forces of the country will get angry, and they can do it, easily, like this, pouh!' All of this will be the doing of the Tutsis, they are the ones that have caused us all of these problems!

"I have told you: Ever since the revolution took place, since 1 October 1990, the armed forces have stayed in their barracks. They haven't bothered anyone, they haven't even looked at anyone sideways. We drink together in bars, the Tutsis and the Hutus, everyone drinks together. They [the soldiers] haven't spat in the face of a single Tutsi, they haven't done anything at all.

"All the Tutsis who we drink with, these are the ones that we call 'moderate Tutsis.' The Tutsis who have values and who are humble, who get along with humans, who work in the ministries, who work in businesses, who go home to their houses, these aren't the ones who run from their houses to go live in Nyamirambo [a neighborhood with a reputation for moderation where Tutsis and members of the Hutu opposition immigrated to escape from the MRND and CDR militias]. But the other truly normal Tutsis, even today, we exchange engagements, we marry into each other's families. Even today, they are godparents to Hutu children at their baptism and Hutus are godparents to their children; there aren't any problems. Anyone who wants to can come to Kigali to see where they spend their days drinking and to see how they are all together.

"Now the soldiers of the RPF, they must understand as well that they [the 'humble Tutsi'] have no interest in undermining democracy. They have no interest in killing their Hutu relatives, killing their Tutsi relatives. These soldiers of the RPF, they should remember that they gained nothing when they attacked Ruhengeri, that they gained nothing when they attacked Mukarange, that they gained nothing when they attacked Mutara, that they gained nothing when they attacked Birunga, etc. The RPF must know that they will have to answer to the people and to history for the youth that they have continued to decimate.

"Let the RPF understand: Before the history of the world, before history and before the people, one day, it [the RPF] will have to explain before the entire human race, how these sons of the country, these good sons of the country, how the RPF led them to their deaths, how the RPF led them right to their deaths. One day they will have to explain. Ha! Rutaremara [RPF representative and official Tito Rutaremara], if you are listening to me, you go tell them, you tell them, 'Hey, yeah! That's the way it is in wartime.' Ha! You will tell them like this: 'That's the way it is with war.' Yeah! Ha! Ha! Blood gets spilled, but it doesn't get cleaned up! [a Rwandan proverb] Ha! There will be news about all of this soon.

"But in fact, citizens, we are calling on you. I often call you the fourth column. The people, you are the real shield, you are the true army of strength. The armed forces may fight, but the people tell them 'We will guard your rear; we will be your shield.'

"The day when the people stand up and they don't want any more of you [the RPF], they will hate you in unison and to the bottoms of their hearts. When you make them sick, I ask you how you are going to escape. Where are you going to go? You cannot rule over people who want nothing to do with you. It's impossible. And even Habyarimana himself, if the citizens don't want him anymore, he couldn't even get to his office. It's impossible. . . ."

RTLM Broadcast, 5 June 1994
(Translated from French by John A. Berry)

Note from the Translator

Ruggio's personal comments that interrupt the reading of the letter are indicated by the use of italics.

"After analyzing the situation all over Rwanda, the Saint Fidele Higher School for Management and Computing (ESGI) in Gisyeni was profoundly moved by the cowardly assassination of their excellencies General Juvenal Habyarimana and Cyprian Ntaryamira, the presidents of Rwanda and Burundi, and others in the presidential entourage. The ESGI takes this occasion to present its sincerest condolences.

"To this effect, the ESGI condemns UNAMIR for its complicity in the assassination of the chief of state. UNAMIR was responsible for security at the Gregoire Kayibanda International Airport and did not protect the presidential plane. Although the Belgian contingent of UNAMIR participated actively in the attack against the presidential plane, General Dallaire continues to say that it was simply an accident.

"The ESGI also condemns UNAMIR for its support of the RPF in the war.

"The ESGI salutes the courage and patriotism of the Rwandan Armed Forces, determined to teach a final lesson to the recalcitrant *Inyenzi.*

"The ESGI recommends that the Rwandan government act quickly to support civil resistance, specifically by distributing the means of self-defense in order to counter the infiltration of the enemy.

"Here I must interrupt to comment that firearms are not the only means of self-defense. There are also traditional means of self-defense,[6] which can be of different sorts. The population must not forget, they don't need only firearms. Surely some firearms will be needed, and we are beginning to have more and more of them, but we still don't have a gun for every Rwandan. This would obviously be impossible. Guns will continue to have their place at the barricades and with security patrols. Don't forget that you also have traditional means of defense. You must get them out and you must use them.

"The ESGI recommends to the government, following the intellectual dishonesty of General Dallaire, that the government should oppose his role in UNAMIR II and demand his immediate departure.

"The government of Rwanda should establish commissions to investigate the responsibility of President Museveni of Uganda in the Rwandan conflict and the responsibility of the Belgian government in the assassination of the Rwandan President.

"The government of Rwanda, through the channels of the Ministry of Information and its diplomatic missions, must quickly deny the allegations the *Inyenzi* and their accomplices have long used to smear the reputation of our country.

"The government of Rwanda must encourage national defense and require every Rwandan citizen to spare nothing to contribute to the war effort.

"The government of Rwanda must react against the unfair United Nations arms embargo and work for its rapid repeal in order to stop the *Inyenzi* aggressor, supported by the Ugandan and Belgian governments, from gaining the upper hand.

"The government must ask our ambassador in Dar Es Salaam to assist the Rwandan refugees who were recently victims of *Inyenzi* atrocities.

"The government must review its diplomatic relations with Belgium and Uganda."

> Signed,
> General Secretary of ESGI,
> President of the Student Committee of ESGI

"We hope you are well and we congratulate you and all the students and workers of the ESGI. Your position comforts us and we thank you for it. And so we dedicate to you the following music. Hot music, good music.

"We also dedicate this music to General Dallaire. The government should oppose General Dallaire's leadership of UNAMIR II and demand its immediate

departure from Rwanda. And you, General Dallaire, we dedicate this music to you to help you to pack your bags and make the only just decision possible, to leave Rwanda quickly. And so, here is some hot music."

Notes

1. The Rwandan government-in-exile was an amorphous group composed of members of the former government, FAR, and the extremist militias. It declared itself the interim government of Rwanda the day after the murder of Prime Minister Uwilingiyimana and two days after the plane carrying President Habyarimana was shot down. Although not a formal government, it held power in the refugee camps by intimidation, force of arms, and control of food aid. The interim government was not officially recognized by any other foreign country.

2. See Collette Braeckman, *Rwanda: Histoire d'un genocide,* pp. 148–49, for a description of the former government's plans to trade Rwandan tea for arms from the government of Egypt.

3. UNAMIR II was created by United Nations Security Council Resolution 918 to replace UNAMIR; its authorized troop strength was 5,500 soldiers.

4. In Kinyarwanda, the singular form of a noun begins with the prefix "mu-" and the plural with the prefix "ba-"; thus "Muhutu" or "Mututsi" means one person and "Bahutu" or "Batutsi" means either several people or the entire ethnic group.

5. Translation of an expression in Kinyarwanda meaning "to have the strength of a lion."

6. The use of "traditional means of self-defense" refers to machetes, axes, and other agricultural tools. During the genocide, the use of these types of weapons was far more widespread than that of firearms.

LEGAL INTERPRETATION OF THE GENOCIDE

Introduction

■ **ANDREAS SCHIESS,**[1] **CHIEF, SPECIAL INVESTIGATIONS UNIT, UNITED NATIONS HUMAN RIGHTS FIELD OPERATION IN RWANDA**

The purpose of this discussion is to provide some information and background on the legal definition of genocide, the legal interpretation of the current crisis, the role of the International Criminal Tribunal for Rwanda, and the approach or response of the international community.

As an introduction, almost three years ago a distinguished aid worker recognized that

> [t]he real danger of the post–Cold War era lies in the proliferation of internal conflicts that kill hundreds of thousands of civilians, displace millions of others, cause unimaginable infrastructural and environmental damage and shatter the frames of political, cultural and economic reference and the system of recourse.[2]

It was not a politician who said this, but an aid worker. He added:

> No continent is now safe from these new style disasters: they can
> knock on any door and there is nothing exotic about them. Their
> victims are simply added to all those of last year's barely
> extinguished and, in reality, still smouldering conflicts. . . .[3]

The author of these statements, Frédéric Maurice, was killed on
19 May 1992 by mortar fire during an ambush while leading a relief
convoy into Sarajevo. The above-mentioned remarks were made in an
article, published posthumously, entitled "Humanitarian Ambition," in
which he argued:

> [W]ar anywhere is first and foremost an institutional disaster,
> the breakdown of legal systems, a circumstance in which legal
> rights are secured by force. . . . War is not only the instant when
> law breaks down and power is called into question; above all, it
> is the ensuing maelstrom of violence and the sum total of
> incalculable and ever-increasing suffering.[4]

Maurice concluded that "[h]umanitarian action therefore, above
all, is a legal approach that precedes and accompanies the actual provi-
sion of relief."[5] By this he meant that one must persuade belligerents to
accept an exceptional legal order, the law of war or humanitarian law.
It could be said that this article was written to define the role of the
humanitarian worker in a real war and that in Rwanda today there is
no "real war," no raging war, and no internal armed conflict. Most of us
would probably agree with that. We need, however, to go beyond the
mere description of a legal order and take a broader look at how to
overcome an institutional crisis in the form of the breakdown of the
legal and judicial system.

If law is meant to maintain peace and provide tools to resolve disputes through judicial procedures, what then went wrong in Rwanda?
Does law not provide its own medicine for the failure of the legal system, or might it be true that there is something wrong with human
beings who seek to jeopardize the rule of law? It has been through this
sort of painful experience and the horrors of bloodstained history that
mankind has developed the essentials of human rights law and international humanitarian law.

The Right to Life and the Rule of Law

■ MAURICE NYBERG,[6] INVESTIGATIONS OFFICER,
SPECIAL INVESTIGATIONS UNIT, UNITED NATIONS
HUMAN RIGHTS FIELD OPERATION IN RWANDA

This presentation will attempt, in simple terms, to explain international human rights and international humanitarian law as applicable to the situation in Rwanda, concentrating on the right to life as a unifying theme underlying both human rights and international humanitarian law. The focus will be on the substantive law proper, on responsibility for violations of the substantive law, and on the rule of law. It will not deal with procedural or evidential issues.

The distinction between international human rights law and international humanitarian law lies in their respective fields of application. Human rights law regulates the relationship between the individual and the state at all times. Humanitarian law regulates the relationship between the individual and the state during times of armed conflict, with different rules applying to international and noninternational armed conflict.

The most fundamental right enshrined in both human rights and international humanitarian law is the right to life. In human rights law, the right to life is found in Article 6 of the Covenant on Civil and Political Rights,[7] which speaks of the inherent right to life and provides that no one shall be deprived of life arbitrarily.

The right to life is a nonderogable human right. Derogation from or the suspension of certain human rights may be allowed in cases of exceptional public danger that threaten the existence of a nation.[8] The right to life, however, and other human rights such as the right to be free from torture, are nonderogable[9] and may never be suspended in any situation, including political conflict. Political conflict such as occurred in Rwanda provides no excuse, defense, or mitigating circumstance for violations of the right to life.

The right to life may be violated not merely with an intent to kill an individual, but also with an intent to destroy in whole or in part the national, ethnic, racial, or religious group to which the individual belongs. This is what is called genocide, defined under the Genocide Convention[10] as any one of the following five acts committed with the intent to destroy, in whole or in part, a national, ethnic, racial, or religious group:

1. Killing members of a national, ethnic, racial, or religious group
2. Causing serious bodily or mental harm to members of a national, ethnic, racial, or religious group
3. Deliberately inflicting conditions of life upon a national, ethnic, racial, or religious group calculated to destroy the group in whole or in part
4. Imposing measures intending to prevent births within the national, ethnic, racial, or religious group
5. Forcibly transferring children from one national, ethnic, racial, or religious group to another such group[11]

The Genocide Convention also prohibits the following:

1. Conspiracy to commit genocide, or two or more people making an agreement to destroy in whole or in part a national, ethnic, racial, or religious group
2. Direct and public incitement to genocide, or speeches made at political rallies or on the radio or articles published in journals that encourage people to destroy in whole or in part a national, ethnic, racial, or religious group
3. An attempt to commit genocide, or setting in motion a plan to destroy in whole or in part a national, ethnic, racial, or religious group—even if no one or only one person is killed
4. Complicity in genocide, or providing assistance to those whom one knows or has reason to know are planning or carrying out the destruction in whole or in part of a national, ethnic, racial, or religious group[12]

The discussion of genocide in Rwanda contains two common misconceptions. First, some people argue that the conflict in Rwanda was political in nature because the former government was fighting against the Rwandan Patriotic Front, and that since membership in a political group is not protected under the Genocide Convention, genocide did not occur. This is an incorrect interpretation, because the destruction of an ethnic group may be undertaken for political motives. In fact, it would be difficult to conceive of a genocide that was not undertaken for political motives. The identification of an ethnic group as an enemy that must be wiped out for political reasons is exactly what is prohibited by the Genocide Convention.

Second, many people in Rwanda have focused their attention on the question of the number of Tutsis killed and have bandied about various estimates of the number of people who died in the genocide. For example, I recently saw an estimate of 800,000 killed, 300,000 of whom were alleged to be children. While this may serve to demonstrate the horror of genocide through an astronomical number, these estimates are of dubious accuracy and of questionable importance when it comes to the substantive law of the Genocide Convention. While an act of genocide itself requires killing "members" of a protected group, even killing one person may be punishable under the Genocide Convention as an attempt or a conspiracy to commit genocide. Even though proof of hundreds of thousands killed may be useful for evidential purposes, the Genocide Convention focuses on the intent of the perpetrator to destroy a protected group in whole or in part. The degree to which a perpetrator is successful in carrying out a genocidal plan is not part of the substantive law of the Genocide Convention.

International humanitarian law provides rules that regulate the conduct of both international and noninternational armed conflict. These rules are found in the four Geneva Conventions of 1949: the first covering the treatment of wounded and sick in the field; the second wounded, sick, and shipwrecked at sea; the third prisoners of war; and the fourth civilians.[13] These Conventions are supplemented by the First[14] and Second[15] Protocols to the Geneva Conventions, signed in 1977.

In Rwanda, the conflict was a noninternational armed conflict because armed force was used within the borders of Rwanda without known active participation of other states. The rules of noninternational armed conflict, therefore, define the circumstances in which life could be taken during the war in Rwanda. In noninternational armed conflict, the basic rules are found in what is called Common Article 3 of the Geneva Conventions of 1949. Common Article 3 is the same in each of the four Geneva Conventions and sets down the minimum rules of behavior in noninternational armed conflict, including humane treatment for those who are wounded, have laid down their arms, or are noncombatants, without regard to race, religion, sex, birth, wealth, or other similar distinctions. Common Article 3 is supplemented by

Protocol II of 1977, which provides additional protection, especially for civilians, in noninternational armed conflict.

The point of these rules is that, even during war, life may not be taken arbitrarily. Some try to explain the massacres that occurred in Rwanda as a calamity that naturally occurs in war. This is incorrect, as the systematic massacre of civilians violates the rules of international humanitarian law that protect the right to life. War, whether civil or international, provides no defense, excuse, or mitigating circumstance for the massacres that occurred in Rwanda.

Finally, let me address crimes against humanity, defined in Article 6(c) of the Nuremberg Charter as

> [m]urder, extermination, enslavement, deportation and other inhumane acts committed against any civilian population before or during the [Second World] war, or persecutions on political, racial or religious grounds in the execution of or in connection with any crime within the jurisdiction of the Tribunal whether or not in violation of the domestic law of the country where perpetrated.[16]

The definition of crimes against humanity has been broadened considerably in international law over the last half-century and was defined by the Commission of Experts on Rwanda as

> [g]ross violations of fundamental rules of humanitarian and human rights law committed by persons demonstrably linked to a party in the armed conflict, as part of an official policy based on discrimination against an identifiable group or persons, irrespective of war and the nationality of the victim, and includes acts such as the following: murder; extermination; enslavement; deportation and population transfer; imprisonment; torture; rape; persecutions on political, racial and religious grounds; other inhumane acts; apartheid.[17]

"Crimes against humanity" refers to those situations where a breakdown of human rights and humanitarian law occurs such that violations of rights such as the right to life take place on a massive scale.

These are the substantive norms of international human rights and humanitarian law that develop the principle of the right to life. Who, then, is responsible for violations of these substantive norms?

Traditionally, international law recognized only the responsibility of a state. A state may, for example, seek damages against another state that, as part of its foreign policy, has committed, conspired in, attempted, incited, or engaged in complicity with genocide.

In addition, the development of individual responsibility in international law has advanced significantly since the Nuremberg Tribunal. Today, individuals who violate international human rights and international humanitarian law may be held individually responsible. This applies both to those within and outside Rwanda. Rwanda is part of the international community, so Rwanda and Rwandans are subject to the legal rules that protect the right to life. But the members of the international community, including those who in the application of their country's foreign policy conspired in or engaged complicity in genocide, are also subject to these legal rules.

Various justifications are often advanced to excuse participation in the genocide, such as "I was told to kill." Superior orders, however, may not be pled as a defense to genocide.[18] One cannot say, "I was told to kill" and escape responsibility, because there is a duty to resist an illegal order. On the other hand, duress, or "I was forced to kill," can be both a mitigating circumstance and a defense if proven by an otherwise responsible party. To distinguish between orders willingly obeyed and duress, however, a defendant is required to prove direct and immediate threat of serious bodily harm or death if the defendant refused to carry out the order.

Legal norms protecting the right to life are an essential element of the development of the rule of law in Rwanda. As the constitutional documents of the government of Rwanda refer to the establishment of the rule of law, it is important to understand what the rule of law means and what its role is in protecting the right to life. The rule of law means that decisions taken by those who hold power are not to be made at the discretion or whim of the office holder but rather according to legal rules. In other words, the law is the sole source of governmental authority.

The development of the rule of law over the rule of power occurs not just in the constitutional documents or the legal system of a country but also in the minds of its people. In his book *Equality*, British author R. H. Tawny says,

Power is both awful and fragile. It can dominate a continent only in the end to be blown down by a whisper. To destroy it, nothing more is required than to be indifferent to its threats and to prefer other goods to those which it promises. Nothing less, however, is required also.

A Hope for the End of Impunity in Rwanda: The International Criminal Tribunal for Rwanda

■ ANDREAS SCHIESS[19], CHIEF, SPECIAL INVESTIGATIONS UNIT, UNITED NATIONS HUMAN RIGHTS FIELD OPERATION IN RWANDA

It is important to mention what a momentous thing it is that the International Criminal Tribunal for Rwanda[20] has been created. It is only the second international criminal tribunal since the establishment of the United Nations, apart from the Nuremberg trials after World War II.[21] The first international criminal tribunal was set up to deal with the crisis in former Yugoslavia.[22]

In this context, it should be noted that the Security Council established a Commission of Experts in the summer of 1994[23] to analyze and report on what happened in Rwanda and to make recommendations to the Security Council.[24] The Commission of Experts for Rwanda has finished its work and no longer exists, but through Security Council Resolution 955 the International Criminal Tribunal for Rwanda was established. It consists of two trial chambers, an appellate chamber, a registry, and a prosecutor.[25] The prosecutor of the International Criminal Tribunal for Yugoslavia, Justice Richard Goldstone, is also the prosecutor of the International Criminal Tribunal for Rwanda.[26]

To explain the tribunal, it is essential to go into detail, and I will have to quote from the statute. First, we must look at the competence of the international criminal tribunal as defined in Article 1 of the Statutes of the International Criminal Tribunal for Rwanda:

> [T]he International Criminal Tribunal for Rwanda shall have the power to prosecute persons responsible for serious violations of international humanitarian law committed in the territory of Rwanda and Rwandan citizens responsible for such violations committed in the territory of neighboring states, between

1 January 1994 and 31 December 1994, in accordance with the provisions of the present Statute.

The territorial and temporal limitations of the tribunal are further defined by Article 7:

[T]he territorial jurisdiction of the International Criminal Tribunal for Rwanda shall extend to the territory of Rwanda including its land surface and airspace as well as to the territory of neighboring States in respect to serious violations of international humanitarian law committed by Rwandan citizens. The temporal jurisdiction of the International Criminal Tribunal for Rwanda shall extend to a period beginning on 1 January 1994 and ending on 31 December 1994.

The second important point is personal jurisdiction, defined in Article 5: "[T]he International Criminal Tribunal for Rwanda shall have jurisdiction over natural persons pursuant to the provisions of the present Statute." In other words, defendants indicted by the tribunal must be individuals rather than states or corporations.

Individual criminal responsibility is defined in Article 6 as

[a] person who planned, instigated, ordered, committed or otherwise aided or abetted in the planning, preparation or execution of a crime referred to in Articles 2 to 4 of the present Statute shall be individually responsible for the crime.

Paragraph 2 continues:

[T]he official position of any accused person, whether as Head of State or Government, or as responsible Government official, shall not relieve such person of criminal responsibility, nor mitigate punishment.

Paragraph 3 states:

[T]he fact that any acts referred to in Articles 2 to 4 of the present Statute [were] committed by a subordinate does not relieve his or her superior of criminal responsibility if he or she knew, or had reason to know, that the subordinate was about to commit such acts, or had done so, and the superior failed to take the necessary and reasonable measures to prevent such acts from occurring, or to punish the perpetrators thereof.

Paragraph 4 concludes:

The fact that an accused person acted pursuant to an order of a Government or a superior shall not relieve him or her of criminal responsibility, but may be considered in mitigation of punishment if the International Criminal Tribunal for Rwanda determines that justice so requires.

The next important point is that of concurrent jurisdiction, as defined in Article 8, Paragraph 1:

The International Criminal Tribunal for Rwanda and national courts shall have concurrent jurisdiction to prosecute persons for serious violations of international humanitarian law committed in the territory of Rwanda and Rwandan citizens for such violations committed in the territory of neighboring states, between 1 January 1994 and 31 December 1994.

Paragraph 2 states:

The International Criminal Tribunal for Rwanda shall have primacy over the national courts of all states. At any stage of the procedure, the International Criminal Tribunal for Rwanda may formally request national courts to defer to its competence in accordance with the present Statute and the Rules of Procedure and Evidence of the International Criminal Tribunal of Rwanda.

Another very important point to make is *non bis in idem*, as defined in Article 9, Paragraph 1:

No person shall be tried before a national court for acts constituting serious violations of international humanitarian law under the present Statute, for which he or she has already been tried in by the International Criminal Tribunal for Rwanda.

Paragraph 2 states:

A person who has been tried by a national court for acts constituting serious violations of international humanitarian law may be subsequently tried only if

a. The act for which he or she was tried was characterized as an ordinary crime; or

b. The national court proceedings were not impartial or independent, were designed to shield the accused from international criminal responsibility, or the case was not diligently prosecuted.

Paragraph 3 concludes:

In considering the penalty to be imposed on a person convicted of a crime under the present Statute, the International Criminal Tribunal for Rwanda shall take into account the extent to which any penalty imposed by a national court on the same person for the same act has already been served.

One question that is often brought up is that of penalties. The article on punishment is Article 23:

The penalty imposed by the Trial Chamber shall be limited to imprisonment. In determining the terms of imprisonment the Trial Chamber shall have recourse to the general practice regarding prison sentences in the courts of Rwanda.

Paragraph 2 states:

In imposing the sentences, the Trial Chamber shall take into account such factors as the gravity of the offense and the individual circumstances of the convicted person.

Last, Article 28 defines cooperation and judicial assistance by states to the tribunal:

States shall cooperate with the International Criminal Tribunal for Rwanda in the investigation and prosecution of persons accused of committing serious violations of international humanitarian law.

Paragraph 2 continues:

States shall comply without undue delay with any request for assistance or an order issued by a Trial Chamber including but not limited to

a. The identification and location of persons

b. The taking of testimony and production of evidence

c. The service of documents
d. The arrest or detention of persons
e. The surrender or the transfer of the accused to the
   International Criminal Tribunal for Rwanda

These are the most important articles of the Statute of the International Criminal Tribunal for Rwanda.

Much has been written about the problems of impunity in Rwanda. The international criminal tribunal is an attempt, however slow, to end impunity. It will send a signal to all those alleged to have committed serious violations of international law, who, in fleeing, think that they have found a safe haven where their impunity will continue. The international criminal tribunal thus upholds the rule of law on an international scale. If law is intended to provide and maintain peace, it has to be enforced. Otherwise, there will be breakdowns such as occurred in Rwanda.

We must also point out what the international criminal tribunal cannot do. It cannot substitute for an effort to organize and reestablish the judicial system in Rwanda. The government of Rwanda and its leaders are responsible for setting up and running the judicial system. The system must provide for a fair and just trial in accordance with international human rights law. We, as members of the international community, need to think about how the Rwandan government and judicial system will cope with the sheer enormity of what happened here and whether there are ways the international community can assist in these efforts.

One should not expect too much from the international community. There is no substitute for the Rwandan judicial system's dealing with the genocide. Rwanda must build up its own judicial system, or the Rwandan people will be disappointed.

The international criminal tribunal can only give signals; it is far from perfect. Even if it functions to the best of expectations, it will be able to try only a small number of cases. The vast majority of cases will be handled in the national courts. If one assumes that 20,000 cases are to be tried, 19,950 will be dealt with by the national courts and only 50 by the international criminal tribunal.

It is useful to shift the discussion from law to politics. We need to think about the following questions. First, the question of the "innocent criminal" has to be answered. There is no innocent criminal: one is either a criminal or is innocent. The criminal is guilty to the extent that he has participated, and to the extent of his intentions.

The second question is whether there is a right to intervene. This is both a highly political and a very legal question. Until the international community sits down to discuss this question and comes to some sort of agreement, there will be no progress on this issue.

The international system is based on sovereign states; there is no such thing as a supreme power in the international community. Because of this, the international community can say that there is no right to intervene in Rwanda. The international community could say that it was an internal conflict and that to intervene would be interfering in the sovereignty of the government of Rwanda. The basic question remains: Is there a right to intervene and under what conditions?

In conclusion, the tasks of the international community can be defined as follows:

1. To report on what has happened in Rwanda in order to keep alive the memory of the genocide
2. To monitor and to assess events in an independent and impartial manner, including progress in developing the rule of law and the activities of the various NGOs, the ICRC and even, or especially, the United Nations itself
3. To assist the authorities in Rwanda in carrying out their enormous judicial task, tackling the problem of impunity

This will require an independent assessment of the needs of Rwanda and an assistance program tailored to the most urgent of those needs. Assistance should be determined by the needs of Rwanda and not by the means available. As Frédéric Maurice argued,

Plausible action to tackle and heal suffering everywhere will call for collective decisions and the carefully concerted mobilization of the means, techniques and resources of all the agencies concerned. . . . All that counts will be the real courage, determination and the professionalism required to intervene in theatres of operation which . . . are fading from the spheres of interest and solidarity of our world.[27]

▉ MAJOR FRANK RUSAGARA, PUBLIC AFFAIRS OFFICER, RWANDAN PATRIOTIC ARMY

I would like to make the following observations. The first is that at the same time the International Criminal Tribunal in The Hague was trying war crimes that occurred in Yugoslavia, genocide was taking place in Rwanda. What was the impact of the International Criminal Tribunal for Yugoslavia on Rwanda? Was it a deterrent to the people who committed the genocide?

The international tribunal will sit outside Rwanda in trying these cases. Its proceedings will be in a language other than Kinyarwanda: French, English, or some other international language. How will the immediate victims of the genocide in Rwanda see justice done? Will they go to The Hague or to some other international capital to listen to trials in another language? How will the proceedings of the international tribunal, held outside Rwanda in a language many Rwandans don't understand, serve as a deterrent to the people who perpetrated the genocide in Rwanda and who still believe that they committed heroic acts as their duty to the nation, these people in Goma, in Benaco and Bukavu?

In the former Yugoslavia, the perpetrators of the genocide are still beating their chests and proclaiming their "heroism." We need to have a mechanism to force these people out in the open. The international community may not be able to manage this task because of other commitments and donor fatigue, but if they do not, it will be a crime against humanity. The people of Rwanda demand justice. Justice must be done and be done out in the open.

▉ ANDREAS SCHIESS, CHIEF, SPECIAL INVESTIGATIVE UNIT, UNITED NATIONS HUMAN RIGHTS FIELD OPERATION IN RWANDA

The first question was, what was the impact of the International Criminal Tribunal for Yugoslavia on Rwanda? I am not an official of the tribunal, but I can try to answer this question. I think that the International Criminal Tribunal for Yugoslavia had a bad start. It still has ongoing problems. For example, a recent op-ed piece in the *International Herald Tribune*[28] stated that the problem of the tribunal is one of money. Justice Goldstone came on the job in August and his investigators are now in the field, but more are urgently needed.

For 1995 he has asked the United Nations for $11.5 million. In comparison, the Iran-Contra investigations, which investigated only about a dozen readily identified U.S. political figures, cost more than $40 million.

It is in many ways a question of money. You have to have personnel and you have to have a budget. It is clear that investigating the genocide in Rwanda is a major undertaking that will require extensive resources. If these resources are not available, this will be a tremendous constraint, one that could even cause the failure of the tribunal's mission.

The victims are very often the ones who are left out. I think the victims will see justice done first and foremost by the national courts. As I said before, and I may be wrong, 19,950 of the 20,000 accused will have to be tried by the national courts and only 50 by the International Criminal Tribunal on Rwanda, even if the tribunal is granted all necessary resources.

The next question was about the seat of the tribunal. This is a delicate question. The parameters of the decision of where the tribunal will sit were outlined in Article 6 of Security Council Resolution 955, which states that the Security Council

> [d]ecides that the seat of the International Criminal Tribunal
> shall be determined by the Council having regard to
> considerations of justice and fairness as well as administrative
> efficiency, including access to witnesses and economy. . . .

Justice and fairness are, therefore, the two major criteria in choosing the seat of the tribunal. In order to have a fair and just trial on the basis of international law, I do not think it is necessary to have the seat of the tribunal in Rwanda. This court will apply international law, not national law. For justice to be seen to be done, it is necessary to hold fair trials, without fear of influence from people in the street. Finally, I must say that the decision on the seat of the international tribunal is neither with the court, nor with the prosecutor, nor with Rwanda, but with the Security Council.[29]

Concerning language, the official languages of the tribunal are French and English. Of course there will be translators to handle the testimony of the witnesses and of the accused in Kinyarwanda. There will be means available to cope with the problem of language.

As far as the punishment that those found guilty of perpetrating genocide will receive, I wonder whether this will serve as a deterrent to the former government officials who published the open letter *"Le Peuple Rwandais Accuse. . . ."* This open letter states that "the RPF took care to categorize in advance the target groups of its genocide. These being the Hutus in general, and in particular the members of the party MRND or CDR or Hutu Power." This is both a denial and a complete reversal of what actually happened in Rwanda.

The international tribunal is not a panacea for the prosecution of the perpetrators of genocide in Rwanda. Delivering justice to the Rwandan people can only be accomplished by the Rwandan courts, which will try the vast majority of cases. The problem is that the number of suspected perpetrators of the genocide is large and the budget of the Rwandan courts is small. Justice must not only be done, it must be seen to be done.

■ Dr. Paulan Muswahili, Professor, National University of Rwanda

There is no such thing as an innocent criminal. The victims are always left out. I don't think that Rwanda can expect too much from either the international community or the criminal tribunal. Rwanda has to build its own society, to reconcile itself.

We seem to be in a rather chaotic state of mind. Half of Rwanda puts its trust in the international community and the justice of the tribunal, and the other half wants to force all of them out of our country. Rwanda has to start tackling its own problems and stop relying on others to do the work. Rwandans should not expect so much—should not expect solutions to come from outside.

Notes

1. Officer in Charge, Special Investigations Unit, Human Rights Field Operation in Rwanda. These remarks are personal and are not made on behalf of the United Nations or any of its affiliated organizations or agencies.

2. Frédéric Maurice, "Humanitarian Ambition," *International Review of the Red Cross* 289 (July–August 1992): p. 365.

3. Ibid., pp. 365–66.

4. Ibid., pp. 371–72.

5. Ibid., p. 371.

6. These remarks are personal and should not be attributed to the Field Operation.

7. International Covenant on Civil and Political Rights of 16 December 1966.

8. Ibid., Article 4(1).

9. Ibid., Article 4(2).

10. Convention on the Prevention and Punishment of the Crime of Genocide of 9 December 1948.

11. Ibid., Article II.

12. Convention on the Prevention and Punishment of the Crime of Genocide of 9 December 1948, Article III (b)–(e). Genocide as defined above is prohibited by Article III (a).

13. Geneva Convention for the Amelioration of the Wounded and Sick in Armed Forces in the Field of 12 August 1949; Geneva Convention for the Amelioration of the Condition of Wounded, Sick and Shipwrecked Members of the Armed Forces at Sea of 12 August 1949; Geneva Convention Relative to the Protection of Civilian Persons in Time of War of 12 August 1949.

14. Protocol Additional to the Geneva Conventions of 12 August 1949, and Relating to the Protection of Victims of International Armed Conflicts (Protocol I), of 8 June 1977.

15. Protocol Additional to the Geneva Conventions of 12 August 1949, and Relating to the Protection of Victims of Non-International Armed Conflicts (Protocol II), of 8 June 1977.

16. Charter of the International Military Tribunal at Article 6(c), Annexed to the Agreement for the Prosecution and Punishment of Major War Criminals of the European Axis ("London Agreement"), of 8 August 1945.

17. Final Report of the Commission of Experts on Rwanda established pursuant to Council Resolution 935 (1994), para. 135, annexed to Letter dated 9 December 1994 from the Secretary-General to the President of the Security Council (S/1994/1405).

18. Superior orders may, however, constitute a mitigating circumstance when it comes to sentencing.

19. See Note 1.

20. International Criminal Tribunal for the Prosecution of Persons Responsible for Genocide and Other Serious Violations of International Humanitarian Law Committed in the Territory of Rwanda Between 1 January 1994 and 31 December 1994, established by United Nations Security Council Resolution 955 (1994).

21. Charter of the International Military Tribunal, Annexed to the Agreement for the Prosecution and Punishment of Major War Criminals of the European Axis ("London Agreement"), of 8 August 1945; Allied Control Council Law #10 of 20 December 1945; and International Military Tribunal for the Far East of 19 January 1946.

22. International Criminal Tribunal for the Former Yugoslavia, established by United Nations Security Council Resolution 827 (1993).

23. United Nations Security Council Resolution 935 (1994).

24. Preliminary Report of the Independent Commission of Experts established in accordance with Security Council Resolution 935 (1994), annexed to Letter dated 1 October 1994 from the Secretary-General addressed to the President of the Security Council (S/1994/1125) and Final Report of the Commission of Experts on Rwanda established pursuant to Security Council Resolution 935 (1994), annexed to Letter dated 9 December 1994 from the Secretary-General to the President of the Security Council (S/1994/1405).

25. Statute of the International Criminal Tribunal for Rwanda, Article 10.

26. Ibid., Article 15(3).

27. Maurice., op. cit., p. 366.

28. See Thomas S. Warrick, "UN Foot-Dragging Could Make a Sham of War Crimes Tribunal," *International Herald Tribune*, 21 December 1994, p. 4.

29. The Security Council has since decided that the seat of the tribunal would be Arusha, Tanzania, the site of the Arusha Peace Accords.

6

BEFORE, DURING, AND AFTER THE GENOCIDE

Introduction

▨ JOHN A. BERRY AND CAROL POTT BERRY

The experiences and opinions of the different speakers in this chapter offer a parallax view of the genocide in Rwanda, one that changes according to the position of the observer. These experiences were deeply affected by the roles played in Rwanda by the different groups and institutions to which the speakers belonged. Among the groups represented at the conference were UNAMIR, the international community, the Rwandan Patriotic Front, Rwandan women, the International Committee of the Red Cross, and the Catholic Church.

The role that each of these groups played was defined by their values, mandates, and will to intervene. Given the nature of the conflict in Rwanda, many organizations found one or more of these elements were in opposition. The humanitarian values held by many UNAMIR soldiers, and their desire to save the lives of innocent civilians, clashed with the limited mandate and resources given to them by the UN Security

Council. The majority of member states of the United Nations sub-scribe, by international treaty, to the principle that genocide should never be allowed to occur again; yet these same values were com-pletely undermined by the international community's lack of will to intervene while the massacres were taking place in Rwanda. Inevitably, the inhuman realities of the genocide created conflict between deeply held values within the same organization, such as those of humanitar-ianism and the duty of neutrality.

Discussion about the roles of different actors before, during, and after the genocide highlights the difficulty in generalizing and in laying blame. The organizers and architects of the genocide bear an obvious and direct responsibility, but to what degree were ordinary civilians responsible? To what degree were any of the groups represented responsible? These questions have no single or easy answer.

One of the most interesting and emotional themes discussed was to what degree the people of Rwanda themselves, not the international community or the church or even the government, were inevitably liable for the genocide, and therefore uniquely responsible for recon-ciling and reconstructing their country. Morally it is difficult to blame the victims of the genocide for their own deaths, but realistically it is equally difficult to imagine a solution to the Rwandan crisis which is not conceived and accomplished by Rwandans themselves.

The Role of the United Nations Assistance Mission to Rwanda (UNAMIR)

■ **MAJOR DON MACNEIL, LIAISON OFFICER, UNITED NATIONS ASSISTANCE MISSION TO RWANDA**

UNAMIR was sent to Rwanda with a Chapter 6 mandate from the United Nations. This meant that UNAMIR was sent to monitor a peace-keeping operation that was already in effect and that we were armed and mandated to use deadly force only in self-defense and in the pro-tection of United Nations installations. A Chapter 7 mandate gives Security Council authorization to use deadly force to establish law and order and impose peace in a particular country or conflict.

Any authorization for UN troops to use deadly force against the cit-izens of a host country must be given by the international community through the Security Council. At no time during the civil war was the UNAMIR mandate changed to Chapter 7, which would have authorized UNAMIR forces to engage Rwandan government forces or citizens operating with various militias and self-defense groups. Such a mandate would have undoubtedly entailed considerable discussion before the member countries would have given their approval.

UNAMIR was only equipped for Chapter 6 operations. Examples of Chapter 7 operations include operations during the Gulf War of 1990, Operation Restore Hope in Somalia, and *Opération Turquoise* during the French intervention in Rwanda. It must be understood that the UNAMIR forces that were in-country before and during the civil war were equipped only with small arms for self-defense and some heavy weapons to protect installations. In contrast, Chapter 7 forces are sent into theatre equipped to fight. For example, the French forces under *Opération Turquoise* were equipped with a full array of offensive weapons such as antitank weapons, mortars, attack helicopters, and fighter attack aircraft. These forces were adequately equipped to engage either of the opposing forces with a reasonable chance of success. The UNAMIR forces under Chapter 6 mandate were not equipped with those types of weapons.

In the case of Rwanda, very early in the conflict the Belgian contingent was accused of complicity in the death of the president. At that time the Belgians, had they stayed in Rwanda, would, in my view, have probably been fighting against the local authorities, as the Rwandan government considered them an enemy force. That certainly would have caused some difficulties in their ability to operate as members of the United Nations force in Rwanda. Another thing that I feel should be considered is that, in the early days of the conflict, certain countries sent their troops into Rwanda under a specific set of rules or a specific agreement that they made directly with the Security Council. That agreement or set of rules dictated what was expected of those soldiers once they were in the theatre of operations. One has to realize that we had military observers from various countries here in Rwanda who were unarmed and were under a mandate that suggested that they did not need to be armed. That was the agreement that their home country made. It was then up to that home country to decide to arm those observers and use them to fight within the theatre of operations. It was unreasonable to think that the diplomacy and discourse between the Security Council and the host country would not take time.

UNAMIR troops were reduced from 2,500 to 400 soon after the start of the civil war. This decision was made, not by the forces on the ground, but by the international community. The force commander was ordered to reduce his forces and keep only 400 troops on the ground to monitor the situation. At that time, UNAMIR's mandate was changed in an attempt to arrange a cease-fire between the government forces and the Rwandan Patriotic Army and to assist, wherever possible, with humanitarian relief operations in the country.

The UN forces remained under Chapter 6 rules of engagement for the execution of this revised mandate. In addition to working to implement this new mandate, the reduced force was involved in the evacuation of foreign nationals and UN civilian workers prior to the arrival of combat forces dispatched from foreign countries. The UN forces also had to arrange for the repatriation of the Belgian and Bangladeshi troops called home by their governments. (Belgium and Bangladesh had decided to repatriate their soldiers rather than allow them to continue to fight in Rwanda.) The evacuation of the Belgians was a sensitive issue, as they had been accused by the former government of being responsible for the death of the president.

The soldiers who remained in Rwanda at that time were heavily involved in those operations. I cannot speak on the behalf of any of the peace-keepers who were in Rwanda that first week, who were involved in convoys and had to pass through roadblocks when massacres were actually taking place. It is, however, important to note that UNAMIR was still under Chapter 6 mandate in this country.

I would like to turn now to my personal memories and perceptions. I will seek to demonstrate the difficulty the United Nations forces had in dealing with the Rwandan authorities, who were at this time still recognized by the international community and who were acting without regard to international humanitarian law, and with the local self-defense groups who had mobilized against an enemy force they perceived to be present in their neighborhoods. Even UNAMIR had difficulties dealing with those who represented authority here in the country during the war. It is a very strange situation when you are dealing with a high-ranking professional soldier who has been trained in foreign countries, who tells you something on his word, only to realize that his authority means nothing to the thugs on the street.

I will outline some of my memories of Kigali in April through July 1994. I remember, upon my arrival on 18 April 1994, meeting some of the military observers and foreign troops involved in the evacuations and seeing the drawn expressions on their faces as they carried out their duties while civilians were being killed all around them.

I was present at formal discussions where high-ranking members of the (former) Rwandan government gave their guarantee for the safe passage through the city of Rwandan civilians under UNAMIR escort. In one such situation, we were given this agreement by the highest-ranking authority within the (former) government, but the convoy was stopped by drunken militia thugs at a roadblock in complete disregard of the agreement. We would then have to negotiate with one of the *Interahamwe* militia while the others waited to kill the people we were trying to evacuate. No matter who the highest ranking authority was or what assurance they gave, it meant nothing to the militias on the roadblocks.

Agreements for the safe passage of civilians could not be negotiated with the (former) government leadership alone, but rather required the agreement of the heads of various extremist militia and self-defense groups dressed in various uniforms. Each one of them represented a small cell of some self-defense group or a neighborhood. At one of these meetings, a high-ranking official of the (former) Rwandan gendarmerie was shouted down by local members of the *Interahamwe* during discussions on a plan to evacuate Rwandan civilians trapped in Nyamirambo. The evacuation had to be canceled as the authorities could not guarantee security.

On many occasions, we received requests from people outside of the country that we rescue their friends and family from areas of the city where they were trapped. We received many of these requests, and most of them involved going to extremely dangerous areas of the city. We realized that there were up to 20 or 30 roadblocks to negotiate, and that, with only 250 armed soldiers in the entire country, we did not have the forces to go in and ensure their passage to safety. We often heard, after going to a certain home and not finding people there, that the militia and the *Interahamwe* would follow up and enter the house just after the departure of UN troops.

While the RPF had insisted upon a cessation of the massacres as a prerequisite for a cease-fire, on one occasion I had to inform the deputy force commander, who was chairing the meetings, that in fact another massacre was taking place as the negotiations were in progress.

Armed youths at roadblocks guarded neighborhoods and were on many occasions drunk by 1:00 in the afternoon. As a result, operations after this time were limited due to the unpredictability of what might happen at the roadblocks. We were stopped at one roadblock and a boy only eight or nine years old leaned into the truck with a fragmentation grenade in each of his hands. His task was to be part of the "fighting force" of that particular roadblock.

The phrase *"C'est la guerre, il faut comprendre, c'est la guerre"* (This is war, you must understand, this is war) was an excuse for any form of senseless killing throughout the city.

Also at this time, the former prefect of Kigali's bodyguards was disarmed in Nyamirambo by the militia, who then used the arms to shoot into an orphanage.

There were 24 roadblocks in the Nyamirambo area, and as I tried to negotiate my way through them I was often accused, as a Canadian, of being Belgian and then summarily harassed.

One particular source of frustration was the lack of consistent criteria for passage at the roadblocks. A group of military observers on their way out of town on patrol would negotiate their way through three roadblocks and be turned back at the fourth, only to then have to renegotiate back through the roadblocks they had just passed. Military observers sometimes had to bribe their way through roadblocks. Since the military and the United Nations do not provide soldiers and observers with bribe money, the troops had to use their own money.

Radio RTLM announced over the airwaves that the UNAMIR force commander was an RPF mercenary and also accused him of personally shooting down the president's aircraft on 6 April 1994.

The Ghanaian troops were constantly shot at while evacuating people by convoy. Although endangered and frustrated, the Ghanaians would always show up to continue with the operation the next day.

The International Committee of the Red Cross (ICRC) informed UNAMIR and the local authorities that wounded Rwandan civilians who were being taken by ambulance to the ICRC compound were being dragged from the ambulance and hacked to death in front of the

ICRC drivers. This had a significant effect on the force's ability to transport Rwandan civilians in UNAMIR vehicles.

Finally, I must admit that on 4 July, when Kigali city finally fell to the RPF, I felt a great sense of relief. It was amazing to watch how Kigali, after only 72 hours under RPF rule, returned so quickly to a sort of normalcy. There was an immediate change.

■ Dr. Jean Damascene Ndayambaje, Professor, National University of Rwanda

I was among a group of people who were hiding from the former government troops at Saint André Church in Nyamirambo. We tried to call UNAMIR many times requesting evacuation and yet they did not respond. We wrote a letter to UNAMIR on 1 May—about 100 people signed the letter. On 8 May, the soldiers came and killed 30 people. As the war continued, government soldiers came in and set up a mortar that they fired at the RPA. The RPA would, of course, respond. In early June the soldiers came and killed everyone they could find. Why didn't UNAMIR help the hundreds of people who were trapped at Saint André Church?

■ Major Don MacNeil

UNAMIR was aware of the request from Saint André Church and was also aware of the situation in the Nyamirambo district. It is important to remember here the size of the UNAMIR force left in Rwanda. There were about 250 armed UNAMIR troops who were already deployed protecting Rwandan civilians who had taken shelter at UNAMIR installations at the Amohoro Stadium, the Mille Collines Hotel, the Hotel Meridien, the King Fayçal Hospital, and the Kigali Airport.

Negotiations with the authorities had been conducted to arrange an evacuation from Saint André Church. Many *Interahamwe* and militias in the area were against the evacuation, and a previous rescue operation at the Mille Collines Hotel had almost resulted in disaster. A UNAMIR military observer had visited the site with a representative of the prefect of Kigali's office. Upon arrival, the official's bodyguard was disarmed by drunken militia members who then used his gun to fire into an orphanage in the area, as they thought an evacuation operation was in progress. A foreign journalist accompanying the party was shot and seriously wounded.

It is important to remember that the Nyamirambo district had 24 roadblocks manned by armed militias. The district is congested and very narrow—in other words, an excellent ambush area for a convoy. Fighting was also raging at close quarters between the opposing forces. Any decision for an evacuation operation had to be based on its chances of success. We felt that it would require the entire armed force of UNAMIR if we had to fight through the area to evacuate those people. There was also a requirement for a truce in the area that we were unable to obtain. The decision not to deploy was based not only on the risk to the force, but also on the possibility that the passengers in the vehicle would be killed in any attempt to fight through the district to safety.

■ Dr. Jean Damascene Ndayambaje

My point is that even at the time that the letter was written by those stranded in Saint André, the UNAMIR forces had come to evacuate the white missionaries who were next door. Is this Chapter 6 applied to some and not to others when it comes to evacuation?

■ Major Don MacNeil

I knew of no operation planned by UNAMIR to rescue only the white missionaries from Saint André Church. UNAMIR knew that there were two white priests in the area when the fighting began. One of my colleagues, a military observer, was with the representative from the prefect's office on the day the journalist was shot. A white missionary helped the UNAMIR military observer place the wounded journalist in a UNAMIR vehicle and remained in the vehicle when it left the area. This missionary stated that when Saint André Church was attacked, two other white missionaries fled to the ICRC hospital, from where they were brought to UNAMIR headquarters the next day. Both were subsequently interviewed by the international press at UNAMIR headquarters. This is all that I know about the white missionaries who escaped from Saint André Church.

I would also like to add a point on the force commander, General Dallaire. When his force was to be reduced from 2,500 to 400 people, he had two choices. He could have barricaded his troops in the head-quarters at the Amahoro Hotel, sandbagged the building, and done nothing but watch what was happening. His other option was to do what he could with the limited forces available to him. He chose the latter.

The force arranged for a transfer of endangered Rwandans between the front lines, attempted to negotiate a cease-fire, guarded citizens who had sought protection at UNAMIR installations, and monitored the security of endangered Rwandan civilians, as guaranteed by the authorities, in areas of the city threatened by *Interahamwe* and militias. The international community must remember that there were only 400 UN troops covering the entire country of Rwanda. The force commander had been promised additional troops, and the troops in place eagerly awaited their arrival, but none arrived until the war was over.

The Role of the International Community

■ CHARLES PETRIE, DEPUTY DIRECTOR,
UNITED NATIONS RWANDA EMERGENCY OFFICE

What happened in Rwanda was the ultimate form of organized and calculated crime—genocide. It was the attempt by a few political extremists to eliminate, systematically and ruthlessly, members of a different ethnic group for the simple reason that they were born, and to kill individuals of their own group who disagreed with them.

After much hesitation and convoluted procrastination, the international community finally acknowledged the nature of the crime, but then did nothing. They not only abandoned the Tutsis to their fate, but also destroyed the belief that the world community would, once the act was recognized, never again allow genocide to be committed. It is sad to see how easily this erosion of the international community's moral responsibility has been accepted, how simply a conviction has been transformed into an illusion.

Is the end of this century going to usher in a new era of indifference toward the suffering of others? More frightening, does the world's inaction in Rwanda, following recent failures in Somalia and the paralysis in ex-Yugoslavia, send a signal that the international community cannot handle, or does not have the will to respond to, killings of this nature and on this scale? What inheritance are we preparing for our children? What values can we now teach them?

The day before I started with the UNREO I finished 20 months in Somalia, where I was part of UNASOM (the United Nations Assistance Mission to Somalia). I was also heavily involved there with the issue of the application of Chapter 7. It was fascinating to see the extent to which Somalia destroyed any ambition on the part of the international community to intervene in Rwanda. What Somalia did for Rwanda was to significantly narrow the options that the international community was willing to consider. The images of the body of one American soldier being dragged through the streets of Mogadishu closed everything off. It created a world of neoisolationism.

In Rwanda, it was only when hundreds of thousands of Rwandans fled to Tanzania and then nearly one million more to Zaire, on specific instructions from their leadership—the very leadership that master-minded the genocide—that the international community mobilized. These people had calculated, correctly, that the international commu-nity would respond to a massive refugee flow in accordance with international conventions governing refugees.

Once mobilized, the world showed itself unable or unwilling to take the necessary steps to somehow identify, if not to isolate, the guilty parties among the refugees. As a result, the perpetrators of the genocide continued, until quite recently, to enjoy the special status of refugees. Worse still, they controlled the food, medical, and other assistance sent to the refugees. These people remain devoid of any remorse; many even hold senior positions with international relief organizations. Some credit should go to the few relief organizations which, after some delay, have expressed their abhorrence to this blind delivery of assistance and have withdrawn from the refugee camps (notably International Rescue Committee and *Médecins Sans Frontières*).

But Rwanda is not the only victim of genocide. For the first time since the term's creation, the word "genocide" was invoked, and noth-ing followed. Following the horrors of the Second World War, states had agreed, by international convention, that they would intervene should genocide ever occur again. It is disconcerting to see how easily the word is now brandished with no effect.

I remember being at the Sainte Famille Church where the Sisters of Charity were working. They were continually harassed and were convinced that they would be killed the next day by the *Interahamwe* because they were hiding the family of a Tutsi minister who had been killed. I later used this moving discussion with the Sisters as entry to encourage Brian Atwood, the head of USAID (the United States Agency for International Development), and General Dallaire of UNAMIR to meet in Nairobi. It was the first time that Dallaire had left Kigali. At the meeting I pushed very hard to get international assistance for Rwanda. It was fascinating to see how much support, compassion, and willingness to give there was at the time.

All we were asking for was the deployment of the remaining portion of the Ghanaian battalion of UNAMIR troops. At the meeting much was promised. All that was needed were 30 armored personnel carriers (APCs) to defend Sainte Famille Church and other areas. But by the time the APCs eventually arrived, it was August. They were delayed because they had to be taken out of mothballs in Germany and painted white, and APC drivers had to be trained. There were delays in the Security Council as they debated a resolution in May to send the additional 5,500 troops. Some of our international partners in the Security Council refused to ratify the resolution because they wanted greater clarification as to the rules of engagement for these troops. Because of all of these delays, the troops did not come until August.

In the Cold War world, everything regarding humanitarian operations was decided by the two blocs. Since 1989, things have changed dramatically. That is why Somalia was such a unique opportunity. A number of us volunteered to go to Somalia because it was the first time the international community was willing to let go of the concept of the primacy of national sovereignty, and the "right to intervene" became the order of the day. The problem is that Somalia was a massive disaster, as everyone now agrees. That massive disaster meant that when the genocide in Rwanda started, no one would consider intervention. My point is that Rwanda is the price of the failure of Somalia. Had Somalia not existed, I think there would have been an intervention in Rwanda. It would have been very easy to intervene, but no one did so until it was too late. It wasn't UNAMIR that let Rwanda down, it was the international community. UNAMIR was not allowed to intervene.

If Chapter 7 typifies Somalia and genocide typifies Rwanda, what will be the price of our failure to address the issue of genocide in Rwanda? The Security Council should be prepared to answer this question on behalf of the governments that it represents. If the international community fails to respond to genocide in Rwanda, we will have taken one step further away from any meaningful humanitarian intervention.

The future of Rwanda is in the hands of the Rwandans. But if we don't address the issue of genocide, if genocide is allowed to go unpunished, then there is no hope. Rwandans have to resolve their own problems because, in two years' time, if *Interahamwe* come over the border from the camps, I am willing to bet that you will not see a single international soldier here. People will have said that Somalia was the failure of Chapter 7, and Rwanda was its price. If the failure of Rwanda is that genocide becomes an acceptable standard of behavior, what will its price be? Rwanda, if we do not do anything, will become the standard for the level of horror that the international community is willing to accept and do nothing about.

I often reflect on the absurdity of the whole situation. In early June, I was watching CNN in Bujumbura (Burundi) the night before I was to come back to Rwanda. There were extensive commentaries on the 50th anniversary celebrations of the Normandy invasion of 1944. The announcer was saying that this was the moment when the international community confronted evil and stopped the Holocaust. Afterwards, there was brief coverage of Rwanda; so many people killed, the horror continues. The juxtaposition was incredibly surrealistic. Not only were they showing the genocide in Rwanda live and direct, but one didn't even need to make the intellectual effort to refer to the past, because the reference was made at the same time on the same television station. And still the international community did nothing. In the future, the cost of our failure in Rwanda will be even greater than the cost of our failure in Somalia.

The international community has a fantastic responsibility in the response to the genocide in Rwanda. I sat and listened to the former prefect of Kibuye, Dr. Clement Kayieshema, for two hours in a refugee camp in Bukavu. He told me about massacres I had never heard of, but that have since been confirmed. And as we speak he is working for a religiously affiliated international humanitarian organization.[1]

The problem is that we continue to defend our staff members even if we don't know whether they are guilty or innocent. There are NGOs that have helped to hide Rwandan staff members who are openly implicated in the genocide. We have the moral responsibility to be politically astute. We can't feel sorry for someone who has committed genocide. Dr. Kayieshema has no remorse. He hates the Tutsis, so he feels no remorse for the atrocities he committed. He said he will come back with the MRND the same way the RPF did, but added that it will not take the MRND 30 years to make their comeback.

Unless we deal with this problem, the international community will continue to unwittingly contribute to perpetuation of the genocide. People shake hands with Dr. Kayieshema, see him as a savior of men, and openly congratulate his successes. It is not only the NGO that hired him that is in question, but everyone.

■ THOMAS KAMILINDI, JOURNALIST, RADIO AGATASHA

We appreciated what UNAMIR tried to do during the genocide, like protecting certain of our leaders. Despite this protection, many of them were killed in the end. I can't excuse what the international community did or didn't do, but let's look at things directly. Until now, no one has acknowledged our own responsibility, the responsibility of Rwandans in this affair. Who taught us to kill each other? No outsider. What must we do now? In my opinion, as long as we do not accept the fact that this country belongs to all of us, and that everyone who is a Rwandan citizen has the right to live in this small country, we have no right to condemn the international community. We are at the heart of all of this.

If we are incapable of resolving our problems ourselves, the international community cannot do anything for us. We, not the international community, must live with the problems of daily life in Rwanda. What the international community can bring us is support to help us do what we do not have the financial resources to do. But they should only be advisors and donors; we Rwandans must be the implementors. If reconciliation is not possible in this country, if justice is not possible in this country, if we cannot share all of the potential that exists in this country, it isn't worth condemning the international community.

Let's stop killing each other. I am sure that if we start right now to massacre each other again, the international community will leave. They will leave, and will we be able to accuse them again of abandoning us? It isn't true and it isn't fair. Let's stop massacring each other, let's accept each other as we are and then things will work out. It is still possible for us to work things out, it is possible.

Why have we suffered from so much intolerance? Let's ask ourselves this question. What is the source of this problem? I am 34 years old. For years I heard the words Hutu and Tutsi, and I never knew what they meant. In my family I never learned these things. In school I did not learn these things. I only learned that the Hutu-versus-Tutsi split existed when I began to work for the government in 1994. Who invented these terms? We accuse the colonialists of having done it. When the whites arrived here did they really invent these terms, or did they exist before? It was we, the Rwandans, who invented these terms. If the colonialists invented the hatred that exists between us then they should be condemned. But now that we know the source of the problem, let's try to resolve it ourselves. It is we, the Rwandans, who are responsible for what happens.

◼ LIEUTENANT JEAN MARIE CAMERON, LIAISON OFFICER, RWANDAN PATIOTIC ARMY

The victims of the genocide included both Hutus and Tutsis. There was, however, one fundamental difference between these murders. The Hutus were murdered for their political convictions, because they belonged to the opposition parties or to human-rights organizations that opposed the former government's policies. The Tutsis, however, were slaughtered simply for being Tutsis. Even babies were murdered as accomplices of the RPF. The international failure to act cannot be attributed to ignorance, nor the lack of means; the intervention force (UNAMIR) was reduced, encouraging the perpetrators of the genocide to continue the killing while the world looked on.

When independence came in 1959, people sought refuge in churches to escape the killings, but the only thing that the international community could think of was food. They gave us food, but we couldn't stay in Rwanda so we took refuge in neighboring countries. When we arrived there, the international community continued to feed us.

In 1963 there were more massacres. People fled into neighboring countries, and the international community again gave us food. In 1967 there were more massacres, planned massacres, organized by the government and implemented by militias of unemployed youths who had been trained to kill. In 1973 the Second Republic orchestrated more massacres, this time of intellectuals, university professors, and students. The people again fled to neighboring countries. When they arrived, the international community again gave them food. Some of the students also received scholarships to study abroad.

Then in 1990 the war started. During the course of the war, there were massacres in Bagogwe, there were massacres in Bugesera, and there were massacres in Mutura, up until 1994, when preparations for the genocide began. Everyone was saying that the militias were being armed. Many letters were written about this. The international community has received letters for 35 years. That brings us to today. The international community is here again, and again they give us food— food and medicine.

I return to Chapters 6 and 7 of the United Nations Rules of Engagement. During the genocide, most of the 2,500 UNAMIR soldiers were evacuated so they wouldn't be killed. At the time, a woman said to me, justifying the withdrawal, "These soldiers didn't come here to be killed at the end of the earth." To the international community, Rwanda was the end of the earth. During the genocide, the United Nations applied Chapter 6, and the UNAMIR troops were reduced to around 400 soldiers. When the others left, the difficulty of saving people increased. The soldiers who were in Rwanda did what they could, but they were only 400.

The question remains why, after the country was liberated, was Chapter 7 authorization given to *Opération Turquoise*, when during the genocide, only Chapter 6 was given to UNAMIR? *Opération Turquoise*, in applying Chapter 7 rules of engagement, came with helicopters and tanks, ready to *cassé les nègres* (break the niggers) if they felt they had to. Now that there is peace in Rwanda we see UNAMIR again, 5,500 troops this time. And now UNAMIR focuses on preventing revenge killings by RPA soldiers who have seen their entire families massacred in the genocide.

Is Rwanda not a part of the international community? Though we are at the end of the earth, we are part of the international community, and the international community must seek justice here. The criminals who massacred our people are in the camps in Goma, Bukavu, and Benaco, very well protected by the United Nations. Some of these people even work for international organizations and the United Nations; others have escaped prosecution and are living happily in various countries: France, Belgium, Kenya, Zaire, even in Vatican City. And justice drags on. What is the international community really doing for Rwanda if this is the sort of help they bring?

We are speaking about the international community because the international community was there during the negotiation of the Arusha Peace Accords. When you engage yourself to resolve a conflict, you are responsible for the results. Yet while negotiations were going on in Arusha, massacres were being prepared in Rwanda. People were being armed, militias were being trained, with the complicity of certain members of the international community, notably France, which distributed arms and trained the militias. While we were negotiating, the others were arming and training militias. Whose fault was this? Was it the fault of Rwandans? Certain Rwandans, yes, those who were preparing the genocide. Who is at fault here, Rwandans who killed each other, or the organizers of these killings? Rwandans are responsible in part, but why didn't Rwandans kill each other before this? Have there ever been massacres of one million people in the past in Rwanda? No.

Today, Rwanda receives assistance from the international community for national reconstruction, but many organizations are also working in the camps that are controlled by the organizers of the genocide. The United Nations has shown no commitment, beyond its declaration of intent, to pursue and bring to justice those responsible for the genocide. Whose fault is this?

The Role of the Rwandan Patriotic Front

■ MAJOR FRANK RUSAGARA, PUBLIC AFFAIRS OFFICER, RWANDAN PATRIOTIC ARMY

I would like to speak about the role of the Rwandan Patriotic Front before, during, and after the genocide. Before the genocide, the RPF was formed to address the political problems of the country.[2] We are nonpartisan, unlike some of the other political parties. We are an organization for all Rwandans, with the goal of removing ethnic barriers in Rwandan society.

Before the genocide, the RPF was party to a peace agreement that was brokered by the international community, the Arusha Peace

Accords. We have remained faithful to that accord in both letter and spirit. We have formed a broad-based transitional government, a transitional national assembly, we have created democratic institutions, formed a national army, and complied with other provisions of the accord. The former dictatorship in Rwanda and the forces opposed to democracy signed the Arusha Peace Accords only reluctantly and did not want them to be implemented. The dictatorship continued to use delaying tactics to postpone the implementation of the accords, but I won't go into them here.

I will talk instead of the role played by the RPF during the genocide. Immediately after the war started, the RPF knew that genocide was taking place and saw it as our duty to try to stop it, and to try to save those who survived. We fought a war to save the Rwandan people. The war had two fronts. On the first front we had to stop the perpetrators of the genocide from killing the civilian population. On the second front we had to remove the dictatorship once and for all. This we were able to achieve in a period of about three months.

It is unfortunate that we were not in a position to save more of the population. We were able, however, to establish law and order, despite the odds against us. We were able to facilitate the establishment of civil administration very quickly. We were able to facilitate humanitarian assistance throughout the country. We were able to facilitate operations like Operation Restore Hope, even though they were dealing with a population outside Rwanda. We were able to facilitate deployment of UNAMIR, which we consider our partners in the international community. In our task of rebuilding Rwanda we want this kind of partnership. We also want to be as open as possible, and we appreciate UNAMIR's presence in helping us to be open.

Needless to say, during and after the genocide we were faced with a very difficult situation. We have limited resources. It is a difficult task and an uphill struggle to restore law and order in Rwanda after the death of a million people. I have been told that after the Second World War, in France alone there were over 200,000 cases of retribution killings. In the fragile environment in Rwanda after the death of a million people, in the absence of law and order and in the absence of justice, some people have taken the law in their own hands. Although this has happened on an individual basis, it does not compare to the example of France after the Second World War. It is criminal, it is not condoned by the government, and we are trying to stop it when it does occur.

After the genocide, the RPF, along with other democratic forces in the country, formed a broad-based government of national unity. Of course this government excludes the elements that were responsible for the genocide, but essentially it is in line with the Arusha Peace Accords. A transitional national assembly has also been sworn in. We have tried, with limited assistance from the United Nations and certain NGOs, to reconstruct and rehabilitate the country. We are also trying to put an administrative infrastructure into place and rebuild civilian institutions. For those of you who were in Rwanda in July and early August, we appreciate your support in this effort.

The RPF requests that the international community act as partners in redressing what has taken place in Rwanda. We are calling for solidarity and partnership in redressing genocide. We should move forward together, rather than having some institutions that are only observers and monitors, pointing out errors. Rather than being observers, the international community should be true partners.

In conclusion, we need justice. The international community asks us to have justice. Now give us the resources to do this. After justice is done, we can begin again, we can talk about reconciliation, about doing away with the culture of impunity. We cannot, however, do as some advise and forget the genocide and extend amnesty to the criminals. This would be a false start, and it would not solve the problems of Rwanda. The culture of impunity cannot be ended unless justice is done.

Women in Rwanda: The Impact of the Genocide on Women

■ **JEANNE KADALIKA UWONKUNDA, DIRECTOR, PROFEMME/TWESE HAMWE**

Rwanda has just lived through a tragedy that caused more than a million deaths and provoked the massive movement of refugees and displaced persons. For reasons that are largely sociocultural, the massacres specially targeted men. In Rwanda, as in many African countries, it is men who have the right of inheritance and who pass on their name, their family heritage, and their ethnicity to their children. The struggle for possessions (land, houses, furnishings) and for power has therefore been primarily the concern of men and of male children. It is they who are given the right to property and to power.

A traditional expression in Rwanda states that "the hen does not crow in the presence of a cock." Because of this tradition, the women of Rwanda were powerless in their suffering during the genocide. In Rwanda before the war, everything that was done was done without the participation of women. Women did not have a role in the decision-making process. It is, above all, because of this tradition that women were powerless to resist the genocide.

Even if today many women are alone, widowed or abandoned by their husbands, even if they are poor, even if they are traumatized, even if they were raped, they are now more than ever the prime actors in the process of reconciliation and reconstruction in Rwanda. We believe that the women of Rwanda must convince themselves of this role. Women have certain advantages in this regard and should help other women to show their strength in the current crisis.

Today, the social fabric, as well as the traditional moral values of respect, tolerance, self-respect, and dignity, have been destroyed. Women have always been considered as the heart of Rwandan society, as those who reconcile, as those who unify the family. Women were considered as *Nyampinga*, "the ones who welcome those who are tired." Women had the power to prevent their children, whatever their age, from taking part in crimes such as those we have just witnessed in Rwanda. But if one considers the participation of youth in the massacres, one realizes that stronger forces were working against this traditional power of women. In addition to other social factors, politicians, the media, and decision-makers manipulated the youth of Rwanda to the point that women were powerless witnesses to the massacres committed by their children, their husbands, their brothers, their relatives.

When one closely analyzes the conflict in Rwanda, one realizes the extent to which the inequality of social relations between the sexes can be a barrier to peace. Above all, one realizes the heavy consequences this barrier has on the development of the country when huge numbers of women are left on their own to manage their families, the basis of society. It is women in particular in Africa who feel the terrible consequences of genocide, massacres, and war. They are largely unprepared to assume all the new responsibilities that fall on their backs. This is why it is particularly important to reconsider the role of women in the new society that is being built in Rwanda.

The difficult times that Rwanda experiences on a political, economic, social, and cultural level require vigilance and rationalism more than ever before. Women's organizations, as intermediaries between grass-roots initiatives and governmental programs, are called to commit themselves to the resolution of the problems of women in order to build a society that is better able to support lasting development. Those involved in the development of the country have the responsibility to seriously consider the best way to maximize the involvement of women in the development of the new Rwanda.

The women's associations of Rwanda emphasize that before the war, women participated actively in economic activities such as agriculture, animal husbandry, commerce, and salaried employment in addition to doing housework and educating their children. Certainly cultural and economic constraints such as illiteracy, lack of access to paid work, lack of rights to inheritance, and the inability to participate in decision-making weighed on the women of Rwanda.

Today these constraints are greatly accentuated, and women who were widowed, left alone, displaced, or made refugees as a result of the genocide are particularly affected. These women, as earlier noted, represent an enormous percentage of the women in Rwanda. New and urgent problems require a quick and efficient response on the part of women's associations:

- Psychological trauma caused by the loss of direct and indirect family members, rape, and its resulting unwanted pregnancies and the fear of sexually transmitted diseases
- Physical trauma resulting from wounds, rape, and malnutrition
- Lack of housing owing to destruction, occupation, or lack of money for rent
- Increase in the number of widows or woman-headed households with many children or orphans
- Problems of inheritance, especially for women who were in common-law marriages
- Increase in poverty levels due to lack of employment in refugee and displaced persons camps, loss of a spouse or other family

member who assured a subsistence-level income, and a general reduction in economic activity

- Increased risk of exposure to HIV/AIDS through rape or promiscuity, especially among abandoned young girls
- A decline in sanitary conditions due to malnutrition, poor conditions in the camps, and lack of health care facilities in rural communities
- Lack of basic household necessities
- Women held hostage in the camps by their husbands, who prevent them from making decisions for themselves and for their children

In a global sense, the women of Rwanda are traumatized by the genocide, by rape, and by destruction of all sorts. They regret that they did not have the means or the ability to prevent such events from occurring. Those women living in the camps remain the victims of a persuasive campaign of false information by militias and former soldiers, preventing them from returning to their homes. Yet in the camps, the lack of basic necessities (food, clothing, health care) is overwhelming. The death toll among children and mothers is very high. The lack of living space, of schools, of sanitation prevents women from ensuring even an adequate standard of living for their children.

Women who have suffered through the war show a disturbing level of defeatism and despair in face of the future. As a whole, the women of Rwanda fear tomorrow. Nonetheless, with numbers of people dependent on them (their own children, family members, and others who escaped the genocide), women show a certain will to struggle to overcome these multiple constraints. This, once again, points out the necessity for women's associations and other development agencies to commit themselves without reserve to supporting women in the heavy task of reconstructing and rehabilitating themselves and the country.

The Role of the International Committee of the Red Cross

■ **LISE BOUDREAUX, PROTECTION OFFICER, INTERNATIONAL COMMITTEE OF THE RED CROSS**

The legal basis for the ICRC's mandate to intervene in Rwanda was given by the Geneva Conventions long before the United Nations was created.

The first Geneva Convention dates from 1864. This mandate was given to the ICRC by the international community—not by the United Nations, but by the 145 nations who are signatories of the Geneva Conventions. Rwanda signed these Conventions in 1964 and the additional protocols in 1984.

The Conventions protect the victims of armed conflicts, wounded soldiers, shipwrecked sailors, prisoners of war, and civilian populations. The responsibility to protect these people belongs first to the states involved and armies involved in conflict. The role of the ICRC is to support the states and armies in conflict with respect to the Geneva Conventions. The ICRC is not a member of the United Nations community and it is not an NGO. It is a Swiss organization that acts only as a neutral intermediary and attempts to gain access to the categories of individuals I mentioned previously, in order to provide them with protection and assistance.

The ICRC began its activities in Rwanda in October 1990, after the RPF invasion. This was what we call a noninternational armed conflict, which lasted until 17 July 1994. The ICRC tried during this period to provide assistance to the displaced populations. We were in regular contact with the authorities in Kigali and the RPF, and we tried to gain access to the detainees on each side and to the most vulnerable populations.

The ICRC was also involved in training soldiers, among them the soldiers of the Rwandan Armed Forces, the RAF. In July 1993, the ICRC organized training in human rights for all the highest officers of the RAF. The goal was to teach these officers how to train their men in the rules of combat. Humanitarian messages were broadcast to the entire population of Rwanda, and an information campaign was aimed at both sides of the conflict.

Following the events of 6 April, the ICRC was in Kigali, and stayed throughout the war. I was not in Rwanda during that period. The ICRC decided to replace the team in Kigali before 6 April with a new team to ensure neutrality in the events that followed. For those who did witness these events, it was difficult to remain neutral. In August 1994, the ICRC replaced the team that was in Rwanda during the war, again to ensure neutrality.

What did the ICRC do during the war? Some will remember that Philippe Gaillard, who was the chief of the delegation, made several public appeals at a time when there were very few journalists in Rwanda, when communications with the outside world were extremely difficult, and when there was much confusion about what was actually happening in Rwanda. These messages followed the principles of the ICRC, in that they did not make judgments or condemnations, but simply explained what the ICRC was doing. This is an old rule at the ICRC: We say what we do, not what we see. I think that the numerous messages from Philippe Gaillard explaining what we were doing clearly explained what was happening.

More concretely, ICRC hospitals were open to treat wounded soldiers from both the government and the RPF and civilians. During the period when Kigali was divided in two, we were working both at the King Fayçal Hospital on one side of town and at the Kigali Hospital Center on the other side. The ICRC also provided direct protection for thousands of Rwandans who sought refuge at the ICRC compound and whom we were able to save from being massacred. I must also mention that this was possible not because of the ICRC, but because the armies on each side agreed to respect the neutrality of the compound. Although there were violations regarding ICRC nurses, thousands of people in the ICRC compound were saved, despite the fact that we were located in a strategic position between the two armies.

Because at the time Kigali was cut off from the rest of the country, assistance to people outside Kigali was provided by ICRC delegations from neighboring countries: Tanzania, Uganda, Zaire, and Burundi. These other delegations assisted displaced persons who in their haste left with nothing, and who were grouped together in thousands. Unfortunately—we must be honest—in terms of protection, there was little that the ICRC could do. The ICRC did what it could, knowing that if we helped someone in the evening, they might not be alive for food distribution the next morning. The role of the ICRC was modest during these events. We contented ourselves with being present, keeping contacts with both sides, and attempting, with the resources that we had available, to help the victims of this armed conflict.

In following up, today we consider that the armed conflict is finished in Rwanda. We will continue for a limited time with an assistance program providing food, medicine, seeds, and sanitation. We are also continuing a location program that has relayed more than 45,000 messages to family members separated by the war. This program covers not only Rwanda, but also families who are outside Rwanda.

The ICRC also works with detainees. The International Criminal Tribunal for Rwanda was mentioned earlier, but in order for people to be tried, they must be alive. To be alive they need assistance in their places of detention. The Second International Protocol states that people arrested in connection with a conflict have the right to certain minimum guarantees. The ICRC provides this assistance throughout the country, with the permission of the local authorities. The ICRC has also offered to organize training programs in the principles of humanitarian law to the RPA and to UNAMIR.

The ICRC is not a development organization. Unfortunately, the ICRC is not in a position today to support or to help the development of the new government. To remain an independent and neutral organization, the ICRC works with all the victims of armed conflicts, whichever side they are on. Above all, if, in a hypothetical situation, instability reemerges in Rwanda, the ICRC must be sure that it will still be able to work here. To ensure this, the ICRC cannot be seen as supporting one side or the other.

The Role of the Church

■ DR. JEAN DAMASCENE NDAYAMBAJE, PROFESSOR, NATIONAL UNIVERSITY OF RWANDA

I do not present myself as an authority on the Church. I am a member of the Church and an observer of the Church, but not an authority. Nonetheless, I am aware of the role of the Church during the colonial period, during the First Republic, and during the Second Republic.

The position of the Church during both German and Belgian colonization was very close to that of the colonialists in every way. The Church was always as one with the colonizers. The first role of the Church, however, was evangelization. The Church was also involved not just with souls, but with bodies as well. The Church was concerned not just with establishing itself as a spiritual presence in the major cities, but with economic and social development throughout the country.

As such, the Church established schools here in Rwanda. I say the Church, but in truth it was the churches—Catholic, Protestant, and

Muslim. During the colonial period, these schools had a monopoly on education in Rwanda. Even public schools were controlled by the Catholic or Protestant churches. Hospitals, dispensaries, and other social services were also run by the Church, in collaboration with the Colonial Administration. At the same time, the Church maintained a degree of distance from the colonialists. Their relationship has been described as "the alliance between the sword and the cross."

During the First Republic, the Church again followed the questionable principle that because all power comes from God, the Church should get along with any regime that is in power. This attitude was also based on a certain opportunism. The Catholic Church played an important role in the formation of the First Republic. President Kayibanda was helped and supported by the Church, despite the fact that his regime was blatantly racist. In 1925 the Church condemned racism, but here in Rwanda the Church tolerated the racist policies of the government. It continued to support these policies despite the fact that the Church was made up of both Hutu and Tutsi clergy, and that these clergy suffered as everyone else in the country did. For example, during the Social Revolution of 1959, houses were burned, cattle were killed, and civilians were imprisoned. Among those imprisoned were a number of Tutsi priests and nuns.

The Church did many positive things in supporting schools, seminaries, and universities, but at the same time, its hierarchy hesitated to take a position on matters pertaining to politics and ethnicity. In the face of the many injustices committed by the First Republic, the Church used only the weakest of language, saying, "There are no Greeks; there are no Jews; you are all the children of God." The Church spoke in these vague terms and issued vague statements that did nothing to correct the injustices of the government.

After the coup d'état that overthrew Kayibanda, the Church, which had fully supported the First Republic, was just as happy to support the Second Republic. The cynicism of the Second Republic, and the role of the Church in supporting it, was clearly shown during a press conference that President Habyarimana held in Bern, Switzerland, in 1982. A reporter asked about a "reeducation camp" where the government was holding Tutsi girls and young women and where government soldiers would go to rape them. Habyarimana responded, "I am a devout Christian, I even have sisters who are nuns.

I must oversee the morality of my country. Here in Europe women dress as they please and you have 'strip tease' shows. I want Christian morality for my country." Obviously the Church was delighted with this head of state who, in public, declared that he was a devout and practicing Christian. After that he had audiences with leaders of both the Catholic and Protestant Churches who supported him fully, closing their eyes to what was really happening.

After the invasion of 1990, many people were arrested, among them priests and nuns. The Tutsi clergy suffered, just as the civilian population suffered. The hierarchy of the Church was very much pro-government and anti-Tutsi. The lower echelons, however, were against the politicizing of the Church, but they had no voice. The Church was based on a vertical hierarchy and the monarchical authority of bishops who were appointed for life.

Before the events of April, the Church issued statements that the people of Rwanda should work things out among themselves. The Church said that Rwandans should not kill one another, that they were members of the same Church and children of the same God and therefore they should love each other. But behind all this, the Church maintained strong ties to the government, to the point that a Tutsi priest who was nominated to become a bishop was refused because he was a Tutsi. He had already been approved by Rome, but the Rwandan Church invented excuses to not appoint him, and when he was presented to be blessed by the Church, they said there was no way he could become a bishop. The Church also practiced a quota system in its schools and seminaries to establish an "ethnic equilibrium." Those who spoke out to condemn this system either died or were sent to prison. All this shows the extent to which the hierarchy of the Church was on the side of the government.

In 1959, 64 priests and nuns were imprisoned, and some were even killed, but the Church did not lift a finger. In 1990, more than a dozen priests and nuns were arrested by the government. At the time, the Church did nothing to raise its voice about these arrests. Now, there are two nuns and two priests who are in prison, accused of genocide, and the Church is up in arms, accusing the government of injustice when four years before they said nothing. This is not a condemnation, but a simple observation.

After the massive arrests of 1990, representatives from the Church went to the prisons to help the people. The Church was on the side of those who were suffering, but it would not help fight the injustice that sent them to prison in the first place. Instead, the Church organized marches and pilgrimages for peace. It prayed for God to bring peace to Rwanda, while it supported a government that was preparing a genocide.

Before the actual killings began, people had already begun to look to the Church for protection. For example, on 22 February, when a government minister, Gatabazi, was assassinated, people took refuge in churches and monasteries. The first reaction of some priests was to say, "What are you fleeing from? Go back home, you cannot hide here," and they closed their doors. There were other priests, however, who welcomed these people.

The astonishing thing is that when the killing really started on 6 April, everyone left the country, especially the expatriates. Foreign priests and nuns left their Rwandan counterparts to be killed in the houses where they were hiding. For example, 19 nuns were killed here in Kigali when they were left behind to die by the white sisters of their order. The bishops left too. Among others, the bishop of Kigali left, telling us to flee as well, although he knew there were roadblocks everywhere and that we wouldn't be able to get away. Human weakness also existed in the Church.

Despite the culpability of the Church hierarchy, the Church itself also suffered greatly during the genocide. All the churches of Rwanda were pillaged and searched, and as many as 450 priests and nuns were killed. All you need to do is to go to Nyarubuye to see the effects of the genocide on the Church. You can see similar human butchery at Nyamata and Ntamara. Where was the Church leadership? They had all left.

Many members of the Church fled Rwanda when the troubles started, but others stayed and died with their parishioners. There are moving testimonies about priests who died in their churches. One of these stories is about a priest in a parish in the east of Rwanda called Mukarange. There were two priests, one Hutu and one Tutsi. The *Interahamwe* came and said to the Hutu priest, "We are going to kill your brother, but we will allow you to live." The Hutu priest said, "No, you must let him live as well. Why do you want to kill him? What harm has he done you? You can't kill him, I will not accept this. You will have to kill me first." That is what they did; they killed both of them.

As I said, during this period the Church suffered greatly. Churches, schools, and convents are almost nonexistent now. The Rwandan Church is a martyr church, but a martyr church only for the Tutsi priests and nuns, not for the others. Here is another concrete example. At Nyamirambo here in Kigali, we were 18 brothers, among us 12 Tutsis and 6 Hutus. When the militia arrived they asked everyone for their identity cards and separated the Tutsis from the Hutus. The Hutus were taken in a truck and driven into town. The Tutsis were massacred.

That brings us to the Church today: Where is it; what kind of shape is it in? We know that three bishops were killed, many priests were killed, and many others fled the country. There are now about 100 priests and nuns outside of Rwanda, mostly in Zaire. What are they doing now? I went to check up on the priests and nuns in exile as part of my responsibilities, and they told me that they will not return. They said they will come back only when the other refugees come back. And the Church in Rwanda, what is it doing? The Church is trying now to rebuild, but without really knowing where it is going. It is still not clear what the future of the Church will be in Rwanda.

Notes

1. At the time of the seminar, Dr. Kayieshema was a senior medical officer at a clinic run by the Order of Malta at the Ati-Kivu camp in the Republic of Congo despite having been publicly accused of the deaths of tens of thousands of people in the Kibuye region. Dr. Kayieshema's reputation for killing was so fearsome that he was nicknamed "the worker" by his colleagues in the former government for the large number of massacres he allegedly organized.

2. Although the names Rwandan Patriotic Front and Rwandan Patriotic Army are sometimes used interchangeably, the former can refer to the political party, the army, or both, while the latter refers specifically to the army. The political and military wings of the RPF are very closely tied, but when speakers refer to the RPF they are generally referring to the army.

The RPF was formed in December 1987 in Uganda by a small group of militant Tutsi exiles and their supporters. Its express intention was to return to Rwanda and forcibly overthrow the Habyarimana regime. Many key players in the RPF held high-ranking positions in the Ugandan army and had played major roles in Yoweri Museveni's successful battle for control of Uganda. Among those who served in the Ugandan army were Paul Kagame, now vice president of Rwanda and leader of the RPA, who was chief of military security for Museveni, and Fred Rwigyema, who was killed during the early fighting of the 1990 invasion. Prominent Hutu opposition leaders such as Pasteur Bizimungu and Alexis Kanyarengwe also joined the RPF in Uganda. (See Gérard Prunier, "The Rwanda Crisis: History of a Genocide," pp. 73–75.)

CONCLUSION

■ CAROL POTT BERRY AND JOHN A. BERRY

We wrote this book because we felt it was vitally important for Rwandans to speak about their experiences during the genocide. Rwandans need to talk about the genocide in order to validate their experiences, to process their suffering, and begin to heal. We also believe that it is crucial that the international community listen to Rwandans talk about their experiences, because a genocide that occurs anywhere in the world should be a global concern (especially in a situation like Rwanda, where the international community could have easily acted in prevention). We also have an obligation to remember what happened in Rwanda to ensure that it never happens again.

Genocide concerns the international community because by its nature it concerns our humanity. The crime of genocide is an attack on the essence of what it means to be human. Indeed, genocide is mass murder, planned, systematized, and executed with the intention of entirely eradicating a portion of the human race. Genocide is the destruction of a people because they exist. If the horrendous implications of the nature of this crime are not enough to move the post–Cold War international community to act, there is not much hope for a new world order.

If the international community had truly listened to Rwandans before the genocide and truly understood what was happening, they might have done something to prevent it. The warning signs were certainly clear. As long ago as 1963, Bertrand Russel denounced the situation in Rwanda as "the most horrible and systematic human massacres that we have seen since the extermination of the Jews by the Nazis."[1] Thirty years later, the International Federation of Human Rights, among other human-rights groups, described the massacre of the Bagogwe Tutsis as genocide.[2] And that time, the gruesome findings of the international commission of inquiry, including the accusation of government involvement in the massacres, were broadcast on television around the world.

Yet during this entire 30-year period, and up until the genocide in 1994, the government of Rwanda continued to receive international aid, both civilian and military. To an extent that was in many ways unique, the international community had the capacity to influence events in Rwanda both before and during the genocide. For example, it is not hard to imagine how different the situation in Rwanda would have been had the French government placed an arms embargo on Rwanda rather than training and arming the militias and the army. (The French were not alone in selling arms to Rwanda. In the early 1990s, Rwanda signed arms deals with Egypt and South Africa, among other countries, worth $13.5 million. This represents an expenditure of almost $2 per person in a country with a per-capita income of $328.)[3] It is also not hard to imagine the difference that 2,500 UNAMIR soldiers could have made in April 1994 if, rather than withdrawing and leaving Rwandans to their fate, they had been reinforced and given a mandate to intervene forcefully in order to save civilian lives.

Finally, the international community must listen to Rwandans to remember what happened in those awful months of 1994. This means remembering not only the hundreds of thousands of innocent victims of the genocide, but also the commitment, both moral and legal, that the international community made to itself to "never again" allow genocide to occur on earth.

"Never again" is not conditional. It cannot be interpreted to mean never again only among certain people in certain places. The commitment that the international community made was never again anywhere, anytime. As great a tragedy as the Rwandan genocide was, it will be an even greater tragedy if the international community does not reflect on the implications of its own actions and inactions in Rwanda and consider what they mean for the future. The grievous lesson of the Rwandan genocide is that as we enter the 21st century, the inconceivable is still conceivable. What the international community learns from this lesson will have a major impact on how humanity defines itself in the next century and on the commitment that being a human implies.

Notes

1. René Lemarchand, *Rwanda and Burundi* (London: Pall Mall Press, 1970), p. 224.

2. From *Rapport de la Commission Internationale d'Enquête sur les Violations des Droits de l'Homme au Rwanda Depuis le 1er Octobre 1990* (Paris: Fédération internationale des droits de l'homme, 1993).

3. See Collette Braeckman's report in the previously cited *Rwanda: Histoire d'un genocide*, p. 150.

CONVENTION ON THE PREVENTION AND PUNISHMENT OF THE CRIME OF GENOCIDE

The Convention on the Prevention and Punishment of the Crime of Genocide was written in the aftermath of the Holocaust. It was one of the first international conventions written by the newly established United Nations. Rwanda signed the Convention in 1975.

Approved by the General Assembly of the United Nations in Resolution 260 A (III) of 9 December 1948, effective 12 January 1951.

Contracting Parties,

Having considered the declaration made by the General Assembly of the United Nations in its resolution 96 (I) dated 11 December 1946 that genocide is a crime under international law, contrary to the spirit and aims of the United Nations and condemned by the civilized world;

Recognizing that at all periods of history genocide has inflicted great losses on humanity; and

Being convinced that, in order to liberate mankind from such an odious scourge, international cooperation is required,

Hereby agrees as hereinafter provided:

Article I

The Contracting Parties confirm that genocide, whether committed in time of peace or in time of war, is a crime under international law which they undertake to prevent and to punish.

Article II

In the present Convention, genocide means any of the following acts committed with intent to destroy, in whole or in part, a national, ethnical, racial or religious group, as such

a. Killing members of the group
b. Causing serious bodily or mental harm to members of the group
c. Deliberately inflicting on the group condition of life calculated to bring about its physical destruction in whole or in part
d. Imposing measures intended to prevent births within the group
e. Forcibly transferring children of the group to another group

Article III

The following acts shall be punishable:

a. Genocide
b. Conspiracy to commit genocide
c. Direct and public incitement to commit genocide
d. Attempt to commit genocide
e. Complicity in genocide

Article IV

Persons committing genocide or any of the other acts enumerated in Article III shall be punished, whether they are constitutionally responsible rulers, public officials or private individuals.

Article V

The Contracting Parties undertake to enact, in accordance with their respective Constitutions, the necessary legislation to give effect to the provisions of the present Convention and, in particular, to provide effective penalties for persons guilty of genocide or of any of the other acts enumerated in Article III.

Article VI

Persons charged with genocide or any of the other acts enumerated in Article III shall be tried by a competent tribunal of the State in the territory of which the act was committed, or by such international penal tribunal as may have jurisdiction with respect to those Contracting Parties which shall have accepted its jurisdiction.

Article VII

Genocide and the other acts enumerated in Article III shall not be considered as political crimes for the purpose of extradition.

The Contracting Parties pledge themselves in such cases to grant extradition in accordance with their laws and treaties in force.

Article VIII

Any Contracting Party may call upon the competent organs of the United Nations to take such action under the Charter of the United Nations as they consider appropriate for the prevention and suppression of acts of genocide or any of the other acts enumerated in Article III.

Article IX

Disputes between the Contracting Parties relating to the interpretation, application or fulfillment of the present Convention, including those relating to the responsibility of a State for genocide or for any other acts enumerated in Article III, shall be submitted to the International Court of Justice at the request of any of the parties to the dispute.

(Articles X through XIX deal mainly with legal technicalities.)

APPENDIX

LIST OF ACRONYMS

APC	Armored personnel carrier	
CARE	Cooperative for Assistance and Relief	International nongovernment organization
CDR	*Coalition pour la Défense de la République*	Extremist political party responsible for preparing and executing the genocide
CNN	Cable News Network	
CRISP	*Centre pour la Récherche des Informations Socio-Politiques*	Belgian Africa-focused research center
FAR	*Forces Armées Rwandaises*	Army of the former government of Rwanda,

FAR (*Continued*)		responsible for organizing and implementing the genocide
FAZ	*Forces Armées Zairoises*	Army of the former government of Zaire, notoriously ill-disciplined bandits in uniform
ICRC	International Committee of the Red Cross	International humanitarian organization
IDF	Internally displaced persons	Refugees within the borders of the country of which they are citizens
MDR	*Mouvement Démocratique Républicain*	Largest opposition party
MRND	*Mouvement Révolutionnaire National pour le Développement*	Formerly the sole political party under Habyarimana. A major organizer of the genocide.
MSF	*Médecins Sans Frontières*	International medical relief organization
NGO	Nongovernmental organization	
NOVIB		Dutch nongovernment organization that accused the RPF of massacring Hutu refugees
NRA	National Resistance Army	Yoweri Museveni's Ugandan army. Many RPF leaders were former NRA soldiers.

OAU	Organization of African Unity	
OXFAM		International nongovernmental organization
PARMEHUTU	Party for the Emancipation of the Hutu	Extremist anti-Tutsi party that rose to power when Rwanda gained independence from Belgium
PROFEMME		A Rwandan women's NGO
PDC	*Parti Démocrate Chrétien*	Smaller opposition party
PL	*Parti Libéral*	Moderate opposition party
PSD	*Parti Social Démocrate*	Second-largest opposition party
RPA	Rwandan Patriotic Army	Army of RPF, credited with routing the army of the former government and stopping the genocide
RPF	Rwandan Patriotic Front	Opposition party that drove the former government from power
RTLM	*Radio-Télévision Libre des Mille Collines*	Private, government-sanctioned, extremist radio station responsible for orchestrating the genocide

UN	United Nations	
UNAMIR	United Nations Assistance Mission to Rwanda	Criticized for withdrawing at the height of the genocide, UNAMIR soldiers not given a mandate to intervene
UNAMIR II	United Nations Assistance Mission to Rwanda II	Authorized in May 1994 to replace UN troops withdrawn when the genocide began
UNASOM	United Nations Assistance Mission to Somalia	Ill-fated mission that reduced UN willingness to intervene in Rwanda
UNHCR	United Nations High Commission for Refugees	UN agency tasked with protecting refugees
UNREO	United Nations Rwanda Emergency Operation	Established to coordinate humanitarian assistance after the genocide
USAID	United States Agency for International Development	American bilateral donor organization

GLOSSARY OF FOREIGN TERMS

Abiru   Traditional historian of the Rwandan royal court

Akazu   "Small hut"; the inner circle of President Habyarimana

Arbeit macht frei "Work makes freedom"; expression used in the Nazi death camps

Bahutu   Plural for Hutu

Batutsi   Plural for Tutsi

Batwa   Plural for Twa

Cheferie   Traditional chieftancy

Événements "Events"; the killing of Tutsis was described simply as an event

Francophonie   The international community of French-speaking nations

Gukorra   "To work"; perverted by the organizers of the genocide to mean "to kill"

Gusaba ibabzi   "To pardon"; a key step in the traditional Rwandan process of reconciliation

Hamites   One of the lost tribes of Israel; European colonialists mistakenly supposed that Tutsis were descendents of the Hamites

Inkotanyi   "Fierce fighters"; the Rwandan Patriotic Army, formerly a battalion of the army of the king

Interahamwe   "Those who fight together"; the most notorious of the militias responsible for implementing the genocide

Inyenzi   "Cockroach"; a derogatory name for the Tutsis

Inziabwoba   "The fearless ones"; the Rwandan Patriotic Army

Jus cogens   Rule of law

Kangura   The extremist newspaper that published "The Hutu Ten Commandments"

Kwiyunga   "Reconciliation"

Muhutu   Singular for Hutu

Mututsi   Singular for Tutsi

Mwami   The king of Rwanda; in traditional culture, the king was an intermediary with God

Nyampinga   "One who welcomes those who are tired"; traditional role of women in Rwandan society

Paracommando   An elite unit in the army of the former government of Rwanda that participated actively in the genocide

Rwandais/e   Rwandan

Simusiga   "The final attack"; a rumored plot by Tutsis to wipe out the Hutus; it was used as a justification for the genocide

Ubuhake   Traditional system of swearing fealty in exchange for cattle

Umuganda   "Obligatory communal labor"; perverted during the genocide to mean killing Tutsis

Zone Turquoise   A "safe humanitarian zone" established by the French from June through July 1994 that effectively allowed the organizers of the genocide to escape Rwanda

SELECTED BIBLIOGRAPHY

"African Rights." *Death, Despair and Defiance*. London: September, 1994.

Bangamwabo, F. X. *Les relations interethnique au Rwanda à la lumière de l'agression d'octobre 1990*. Ruhengeri: Éditions Universitaire du Rwanda, 1991.

Braeckman, Collette. *Rwanda: Histoire d'un génocide*. Paris: Librairie Artheme Fayard, 1994.

Brauman, Rony. "Protection of Civilians in Conflict." *World in Crisis: The Politics of Survival at the End of the Twentieth Century*. Paris: Médecins Sans Frontières, 1996.

Bulletin Africain. The Research Center on Socio-Political Information. Brussels, 5 February 1960.

Cahiers Africains. *Rwanda, appauvrissement et adjustement structurel*. Bruxelles: Cahiers Africains, 1995.

Destexhe, Alain. *Rwanda: Essai sur le génocide*. Bruxelles: Éditions Complexe, 1994.

———. *Rwanda and Genocide in the Twentieth Century*. New York: New York University Press, 1995.

Dialogue 146 (May–June 1991).

Erny, P. *De l'éducation traditionnelle à l'enseignement moderne au Rwanda (1900–1975)*. Lille: Université de Lille III, 1981.

Fédération Internationale des Droits de l'Homme. *Report of the Commission of Inquiry on Human Rights Violations in Rwanda since the 1st of October 1990*. Paris: Fédération International des Droits de l'Homme, 1993.

Gudrun, Honke. *Au plus profond de l'Afrique: Le Rwanda et la colonisation allemande 1885–1919*. Wuppertal: Peter Hammer Verlag, 1990.

"The Hutu Ten Commandments." *Kangura*, 10 December 1990.

International Commission of Inquiry, *Report on Rwanda*. 26 February 1960.

Joint Evaluation of Emergency Assistance to Rwanda. *The International Response to Conflict and Genocide: Lessons from the Rwanda Experience. Volume I, Historical Perspective: Some Explanatory Factors*. Copenhagen: The Steering Committee of the Joint Evaluation of Emergency Assistance to Rwanda, 1996.

Keene, Fergal. *Season of Blood: A Rwandan Journey*. London: The Penguin Group, 1995.

———. Interview with Gerard Prunier. In "Valentina's Nightmare." PBS *Frontline*, 1 April 1997.

Krop, Pascal. *Le génocide franco-africain: Faut-il juger les Mitterands?* Paris: Jean-Claude Lattès, 1994.

Le Journal de Génève, Interview with Monsignor Parraudin. 17 April 1994.

Lemarchand, Réné. *Rwanda and Burundi*. London: Pall Mall Press, 1970.

Maurice, Frédéric. "Humanitarian Ambition." *International Review of the Red Cross* 289 (July–August 1992).

Ministère de l'Enseignement Primaire et Secondaire. *Dynamique des équilibres ethniques et régional dans l'enseignement secondaire rwandais*. Kigali: 1986.

Ministère de l'Enseignement Supérieur et de la Recherche Scientifique. *L'Université Nationale du Rwanda en 1990*. Kigali: Régie de l'Imprimerie Scolaire, December 1990.

Minister of Justice of the former Government of Rwanda. "The Rwandan People Accuse. . . ." Translated by John A. Berry. Washington, D.C.: Howard University, 1998.

Ndayambaje, Jean Damascène. *Rapports entre l'éducation et l'emploi en Afrique noire*. Fribourg: Éditions St. Paul, 1983.

Nkubdabagenzi, F. *Rwanda politique 1958–1960.* Bruxelles: CRISP, 1961.

Petit Robert. Paris: Dictionnaires Le Robert, 1994.

Prunier, Gerard. "La crise rwandaise." *Refugee Survey Quarterly* (1994).

———. *The Rwanda Crisis: History of a Genocide.* London: Hurst and Co., 1995.

Rutayisire, P. *L'évangélisation au Rwanda 1922–1945.* Fribourg: Editions St. Paul, 1984.

Sylla, L. *Tribalisme et parti unique en Afrique noire.* Paris: Presse de la Fondation Nationale des Sciences, 1977.

United Nations Commission of Experts on Rwanda. *Final Report.* 9 December 1994.

Université Nationale du Rwanda. *Textes légaux et réglementaires de l'Université Nationale du Rwanda de 1963 à 1985.* Butare: Secrétariat Général de l'Université, 1985.

Williame, Jean-Claude. *Aux sources de l'hécatombe rwandaise.* Paris: Éditions Harmattan, 1995.

INDEX

6-05   5|17|05